THE EVERYTHING
HR Kit

THE **EVERYTHING**
HR Kit

A Complete Guide to Attracting, Retaining,
and Motivating High-Performance Employees

John Putzier, SPHR and David J. Baker, SPHR

AMACOM

American Management Association
New York • Atlanta • Brussels • Chicago • Mexico City • San Francisco
Shanghai • Tokyo • Toronto • Washington, D.C.

Bulk discounts available. For details visit:
www.amacombooks.org/go/specialsales
Or contact special sales:
Phone: 800-250-5308.
E-mail: specialsls@amanet.org
View all AMACOM titles at: www.amacombooks.org

Library of Congress Cataloging-in-Publication Data

Putzier, John, 1951–
    The everything HR kit : a complete guide to attracting, retaining & motivating high-performance employees / John Putzier and David J. Baker.
        p.   cm.
    Includes index.
    ISBN-13: 978-0-8144-1609-9
    ISBN-10: 0-8144-1609-8
    1. Employees—Recruiting.   2. Employee selection.   3. Employee retention.   4. Employee motivation.   5. Personnel management.   I. Baker, David J.   II. Title.

    HF5549.5.R44P88   2011
    658.3—dc22

                                                        2010020877

About AMA

American Management Association (www.amanet.org) is a world leader in talent development, advancing the skills of individuals to drive business success. Our mission is to support the goals of individuals and organizations through a complete range of products and services, including classroom and virtual seminars, webcasts, webinars, podcasts, conferences, corporate and government solutions, business books and research. AMA's approach to improving performance combines experiential learning—learning through doing—with opportunities for ongoing professional growth at every step of one's career journey.

Printing number

10 9 8 7 6 5 4 3 2

Contents

Preface

The purpose of this kit is to make life easier, more profitable, and more productive for your organization and its leaders, whether or not you currently have a human resources department, and whether you are a for-profit, not-for-profit, or public organization. Although you may sense a slant toward the for-profit sector in this kit and tools, there is literally no difference in how to become an employer of choice, whether you are selling hamburgers or saving the planet.

If you are a not-for-profit or public organization and you see the word *profit*, just substitute the words *attainment of mission*. If you see the word *customer*, just substitute the word *client* or *stakeholder*. Having taught in the H. J. Heinz III School of Public Policy at Carnegie Mellon University, and having completed graduate studies in the School of Government and Public Administration at American University, I can tell you firsthand that there are few, if any, differences in what you need to know and do to become a high-performing employer of choice, *regardless of your industry or sector*.

Most organizations are sorely in need of better people and better performance. It's not that the people they hire are bad; it's just that they have bad recruitment, selection, and retention processes. As they say, "You can't teach a pig to sing. It just frustrates you, and annoys the pig."

Many of the recommendations in this kit may appear to be "not for you." We hope so, because that means they are things that you aren't doing and probably have never tried. So, please keep an open mind. Just try one thing at a time. That's why there is a fill-in-the-blanks, step-by-step action plan at the end of the kit.

We all know that employee turnover is a killer. But that's just one piece of the puzzle. If we have the wrong people in the jobs to begin with, it really doesn't matter if we reduce turnover. It also doesn't matter if we have the best processes in the world, because they are just words on paper if the people who are to be following these processes are constantly turning over, or if they don't have the ability to follow them in the first place.

This kit, if followed as recommended, will not only reduce turnover, but also improve the quality of the people you select and hire, and their subsequent performance, which has a direct impact on customer/client satisfaction, customer/client loyalty, and profitability (or attainment of mission).

The process is laid out in somewhat of a chronological order (preemployment, postemployment, and so on), but you can still pick and choose what you want to adopt, given the needs, philosophy, and culture of your particular organization.

The first section of the kit makes the case for implementing the initiatives that are introduced throughout the rest of the kit and on the CD. You and your leadership team will never follow through with these initiatives without the motivation to do so. And all motivation is rooted in the *why*.

One of the most common mistakes that organizations and their leaders make when introducing change is to just tell people *what* needs to be done, and *how* to do it. Without the *why*, there is no reason to be committed to it.

Once you have made the case, either for yourself or for your leadership team, we then start small. In order to stay motivated, initially you need to see results rather quickly, easily, and inexpensively. That's why we start with building-block exercises, such as the "Why Work Here?" statement, which then can be rolled up into a recruitment brochure, which can then be rolled into your web site, and so on.

By the time you get through these steps, you will be ready to take bigger bites of the elephant, because you will have some momentum and the satisfaction of seeing results. From this point on, you will see that the kit is laid out in a fairly logical sequence of recommendations, from job descriptions (aka success profiles) to structured behavioral interviews and all the way through the employee-employer relationship, which we hope will be a long and productive one.

We've even taken it one step further. In the unfortunate event that the employee-employer relationship must be severed, there are also checklists, guidelines, tools, and templates for the termination and exit process.

In addition to all of the creative and strategic best practices in HR and management, there are also tons of day-to-day operational processes, policies, and procedures for those organizations that need to start from scratch. We recommend that you open the enclosed CD and browse around. Even though many of the documents and tools on the CD are mentioned in the book, you will get more value from this kit by perusing the CD as well. The CD truly is a virtual HR department in a kit.

OK! Now roll up your sleeves, unzip your forehead, and let's get to work!

ACKNOWLEDGMENTS

Since this is my third book, there aren't a whole lot of acknowledgments left in my repertoire without being redundant or pandering; however, I would be remiss if I didn't acknowledge the continued patience and support of my dear wife, Loriann.

If you read my second book, which was dedicated to her, you would know the story of how she did not want me to write another book because of the toll my first book had taken on me and my family. But, being a rebel, I had to prove something, so I wrote the second book on the sly, to prove that I could do it again without all the negative side effects. That's why it was dedicated to her. She knew nothing about it until the presses were rolling. She knew about this one! Thank you, Loriann!

So, at this point in my life and my career, the only other person I really have left to acknowledge for the success of this book is my coauthor, David J. Baker, M.A., SPHR. It was truly serendipity that we ended up collaborating on this kit, and it was all because we shared a golf cart at a human resources association golf outing.

To make a long story short, I had just submitted the first draft of the book, which was really only about half-baked, to AMACOM when Dave mentioned that he was finally going out on his own and was developing an HR Department in a Box, which is actually what we were going to title this kit originally.

One thing led to another, and we realized the synergy there would be if we combined our efforts. I was the big-picture guy with the weird ideas, and he was the lifetime HR wonk who had built HR departments from the ground up for his entire career to date.

David brought immediate energy, focus, and expertise to the process, as well as a common set of values, philosophies, and professionalism that made this a perfect marriage of two old friends and colleagues.

Thank you, Loriann and David.

John Putzier, M.S., SPHR

Although it has taken me more than 30 years to develop the insight and information that have been compiled here, it has been most difficult to write these acknowledgments. Why? There have been hundreds of people who have contributed to this book, either directly or indirectly, through their counsel, their contributions, and their example.

Professional organizations like the Society for Human Resource Management, the HR Leadership Forum, and our local Pittsburgh Human Resource Association provide invaluable tools and assistance to aspiring HR professionals. Student associations provide a great start in developing students who are interested in entering our profession and need great faculty sponsors. I was fortunate to have Dr. Conrad Gates from Saint Vincent College and attorney John Bechtol from Saint Francis University. You're the reason I chased this profession to begin with. That said, there are a few *special* individuals whom I would like to thank.

My wife of nearly 30 years, Patty, who is my best friend, closest advisor, and the most influential person in my life. My children: David, who is studying chemical engineering at the University of Notre Dame, and his new wife, Sarah, our official second daughter; our son Brian, who is studying civil engineering at the University of Dayton; our daughter Maria, who is studying pharmacy at Duquesne University;

and our son Jared, at Quigley Catholic High School. You are all scholars, athletes, friends, and truly our greatest achievements.

My parents, Anne and John, whose tremendous faith, work ethic, and commitment to their children have molded my life; my sisters, Annette and Janet; my brother Bob, whom we lost much too young; and my oldest brother, who was my original idol, Jared. And just as important, Ernie and Mary Taormina, my mother- and father-in-law. They were an important part of my life.

Mentors, the most important roles that professionals can play in the lives of other professionals, have played a major role in my career. My first mentor, Marty Unger, who advised me to do what no one else wanted to do; Don Korb, retired treasurer of Westinghouse; Lloyd Kaiser and Dr. Tom Skinner, CEO and EVP of WQED; and Jeff Lynn, division president of ADC Telecommunications, have been invaluable in my professional quest for excellence. I could never thank them enough for everything they've done for me.

A special recognition goes out to Lynn Patterson, who has been the most exceptional professional I have had the opportunity to partner with in my career. Everyone should be so blessed as to have someone as talented, intelligent, and creative to work with. She has made me look better than I really am in everything we've delivered and has been a tremendous asset as we started HC Advisors (aka Human Capital Advisors). Thank you for your integrity and excellence in everything you do.

And finally, to John Putzier, M.S., SPHR, my coauthor. John and I have been colleagues for more than 20 years, having worked together designing HR processes and systems early on in our association and as sounding boards on professional challenges throughout our careers. He has been an inspiration, an advisor, and, most important, a friend. I am truly honored to have been a part of this effort and look forward to collaborating on our next project.

David J. Baker, M.A., SPHR

THE EVERYTHING
HR Kit

Introduction: Making the Case

HUMAN RESOURCE SELF-ASSESSMENT

We cannot change what we don't acknowledge. This section will help you and your leadership team understand and acknowledge where you are now, where you could be, and the areas in which you need to focus if you are to become an employer of choice. It is worth taking the time to reflect and assess where your gaps in performance are so that you will have the motivation to move forward—that is, to acknowledge what you need to change or improve upon.

The first step is to complete the brief Human Resource Best Practices Self-Assessment that follows, before embarking on the rest of this kit. (A blank copy of this assessment tool is also on the enclosed CD.) It will introduce you to the concept of "Total HR" and how it is different from the way you probably look at the dynamics of the employment process today. It will also give you a snapshot of where to start and show you your long-term opportunities for improvement.

Ideally, each member of your management/leadership team should complete this survey independently, followed by a team meeting, discussion, and comparison of the results. Then, as you proceed step by step through the rest of the kit, you will have better consensus and focus on how and why to become an employer of choice, and greater motivation to do so.

Note that we use both the terms *management* and *leadership*. They are not synonyms, nor are they interchangeable. At the end of this book, you will learn what the differences are, and how to transform your current "management" team into a "leadership" team. There are tools, templates, and techniques throughout this book and the accompanying CD that address both roles, that is, management (operational) and leadership (strategic).

Human Resource Best Practices Self-Assessment

HR Brand Image	Yes	No
We are considered an "employer of choice" in the communities in which we do business.		
If a stranger were asked what he or she thinks or knows about our organization, the response would be positive.		
Our vendors, suppliers, and customers recommend top candidates for employment to us.		
Our employees are ambassadors for the organization wherever they go.		
Everyone in our organization has business cards.		

Recruitment	Yes	No
We have the "pick of the litter" when recruiting for job openings.		
We are creative in our sourcing (i.e., we go well beyond just advertising and posting on Internet job boards).		
Not only do the best candidates apply, but the majority accept our job offers.		
We pay "bird dog" referral bonuses to *anyone* who refers new hires.		
We use current employees in our recruitment process to help us screen, sell, and select candidates.		

Selection	Yes	No
Hiring decisions are based on more than interviews, background checks, and references.		
More than one person is involved in the interview and selection process and hiring decision.		
We have a formal process for determining why candidates reject our offers.		
Our selection process is a positive and user-friendly experience for the candidate.		
Our compensation and benefits have been validated against industry and community benchmarks.		

Orientation (On-Boarding)   Yes   No

We have a formal new-employee orientation/on-boarding program.

We make an awesome first impression during an employee's first week
on the job.

Our process for bringing employees on board is designed to instill values,
not just teach procedures.

We positively involve our current employees in new-employee orientation.

We periodically reorient all our employees to our core values and culture.

Employee Relations   Yes   No

All of our managers and supervisors are effective human resource managers.

We have a regularly published newsletter that is read and viewed as credible.

We have regular staff meetings that are about more than just telling people
what is wrong and what to do.

We have creative recognition and rewards activities that involve more
than money.

We conduct annual employee perception surveys, then communicate and act
upon the results.

Turnover   Yes   No

When it comes to turnover, we tend to lose the losers and keep the winners.

Before losing a valuable employee, we can usually see it coming and try to
prevent it.

We have exit interviews with departing employees both before they leave
and again a few weeks later.

We actively keep in touch with valuable former employees and continue to
recruit them.

We offer to restore or bridge former employees' service if they return
within a certain time.

Total "Yes" Answers: _____
25 or more = You are an "Employer of Choice" candidate—congratulations
24 or fewer = Look at each category, and for any with fewer than 4 "Yes" answers, identify
opportunities for improvement

CALCULATING THE COST OF EMPLOYEE TURNOVER

If you completed the HR Self-Assessment in the prior section, you now know where your opportunities for improving employee motivation and retention lie. But that's just the beginning. Now we're going to see how much these lost opportunities are costing you in turnover.

If you have been in the employer's seat for any length of time, you already know how painful turnover is, both to you and to your entire organization—not just in dollars, but in aggravation. However, some people still need convincing, so the next worksheet will give you a conservative, real dollars estimate of what turnover actually costs when just one employee leaves and must be replaced. Remember, this does not take into consideration the intangible costs, such as customer relations and stress on coworkers (and you).

For this example, we used the scenario of an auto dealership losing a sales consultant, not only because this is a traditionally high-turnover profession and industry but also because most people can relate to the product and other key variables.

You can use this same worksheet (also on the CD) to plug in your own "real" numbers and assumptions for *any* position. It doesn't matter what industry or sector you are in or what your product or service is; the methodology is the same. The bottom line is that the cost of losing people is staggering, as you will see.

And now for a real eye-opener! Go to your payroll department and ask how many W-2s it issued in the last calendar year. Then ask how many employees you actually have on staff. If you have 100 employees and you issued 200 W-2s, then you have 100 percent turnover.

(Please note that this does not imply that you have 100 percent turnover in every department. We recommend that you drill down, look at each department separately, and identify where the highest turnover is occurring. For example, you may have 200 percent turnover in your sales force and little or no turnover in your office staff.)

Now take the turnover calculator and multiply the cost of turnover for one position times the number of people you lost last year. Obviously compensation is a variable, but this is a simple and powerful (quick and dirty) estimate, and if that doesn't give you heartburn, then nothing will. Want more evidence? Read on.

Cost of Employee Turnover Worksheet

Separation

A　Hourly wage of the person processing employee separation paperwork multiplied by the average number of hours spent processing this paperwork　$　56

Hourly wage of processor	$　28
Number of hours spent on paperwork ×	2

A Separation Expense　$　56

Recruiting

B　Time required to develop help wanted ads multiplied by the hourly wage of the person developing these ads　$　50

Number of hours to develop ads	2
Hourly wage of person creating ads ×	$　25

C　Cost of running the ad　$　1,200

Local newspaper for 14 days	$　450
Online web sites (Monster, CareerBuilder, etc.)	$　500
Trade and association publications	$　250

D Recruiting Expense　$　1,250

Selection

E　Time to review résumés and applications (30 min each) multiplied by the hourly wage of the reviewer　$　240

Hours reviewing résumés and applications	10
Hourly wage of reviewer ×	$　24

F　Average time to interview a candidate (30 min each) multiplied by the number of candidates, the number of interviewers, and the average hourly wage of the interviewers　$　90

Hours per interview	0.5
Number of candidates ×	3
Number of interviewers ×	2
Average hourly wage of interviewers ×	$　30

G　Costs to check references and for background investigations　$　500
$　500

H　Cost of preemployment skill and behavioral assessment　$　200
$　200

I　Cost of drug tests, credit checks, DMV reports, etc.　$　800
$　800

J Selection Expense　$　1,830

Processing

K	Hourly wage of person processing new-employee paperwork multiplied by the average number of hours spent processing this paperwork		$ 120

Hourly wage of processor	$ 24	
Number of hours spent processing ×	5	

L	Cost of business cards, name badges, uniforms, etc.		$ 300
		$ 300	

M Processing Expense		$ 420

Miscellaneous expenses

N	Increased unemployment insurance, etc.		$ 1,000
		$ 1,000	

N Miscellaneous Expense		$ 1,000

Orientation

O	Time required for orientation of new employee (3 hours minimum) multiplied by the hourly wage of the person conducting the orientation		$ 72

Hours spent on orientation for new employee	3	
Hourly wage of person conducting the orientation ×	$ 24	

P	Hourly wage paid to new employee during orientation multiplied by the time taken for orientation		$ 36

Hourly wage of new employee	$ 12	
Hours required for orientation ×	3	

Q Orientation Expense		$ 108

Training

R	Number of hours the employee is being trained at the organization during the rst 12 months (Web-based and instructor-led), multiplied by the employee's and the manager's or the trainer's hourly wage		$ 1,250

Number of hours of training	25	
Employee's hourly wage	$ 20	
Manager's or trainer's hourly wage	$ 30	

S	Sum of hard costs for training events		$ 4,000

Cost for off-site training events	$ 1,000	
Wages paid during events	$ 500	
Travel costs (hotel, meals, parking, airfare, etc.)	$ 500	
Event enrollment fees	$ 2,000	

Training Expense		$ 5,250

Lost productivity

U	Note: Calculate only one position per worksheet (open for two weeks) Sales		$ 10,000

Lost sales while position is open multiplied by average gross profit per vehicle

Number of cars	20
Average gross profit	$ 500

Lost sales due to reduced referrals and repeat sales during the first 12 months multiplied by average unit gross profit per vehicle $ 5,000

Number of cars	10
Average gross profit	$ 500

Service advisor $ 1,000

Lost sales while position is open	$ 500
Lost sales due to lack of trained skills and product familiarity during first 90 days	$ 500

Service technician $ 1,000

Lost sales while position is open	$ 500
Lost sales due to lack of trained skills and product familiarity during first six months	$ 500

Parts advisor $ 1,300

Lost sales while position is open	$ 500
Lost sales due to lack of trained skills and product familiarity during first three months	$ 800

Administrative $ 800

Cost of lost productivity and overtime due to lack of knowledge of organization processes and technologies during first three months	$ 800

Support positions (lot technicians, drivers, etc.) $ 500

Cost of having other employees cover this position while it is open	$ 500

U Lost Productivity $ 19,600

Tabulation

A	Separation expense	$	56
D	Recruiting expense	$	1,250
J	Selection expense	$	1,830
M	Processing expense	$	420
N	Miscellaneous expenses	$	1,000
Q	Orientation expense	$	108
T	Training expense	$	5,250
U	Lost productivity expense	$	19,600
	Cost of turnover for this position	$	29,514

THE CYCLES OF SATISFACTION

Every organization is on either the high road or the low road to employee and customer satisfaction. Take a look at the two cycles in Figure I-1 and ask yourself which road your organization is traveling.

Then ask yourself, of the five components, which one do you have the most control over? If you answered "employee satisfaction," then you are ready to move forward with this program.

We can't improve profitability just by raising prices. We can't satisfy the customer just by having great processes (words on paper). It's the people working the processes that determine whether our customers are happy, and whether we are making money or achieving our mission.

With employee satisfaction comes employee loyalty; with employee loyalty comes customer satisfaction; with customer satisfaction comes customer loyalty; and with customer loyalty comes profitability, which comes full circle to further enhance employee satisfaction, and so on, and so on. And the reverse is just as true. It's usually not hard to see and know which cycle an organization is on.

Every organization has products or services. Most organizations are selling a commodity, in the minds of most consumers. Every organization has computers, equipment, and all of the other *stuff* it needs in order to operate. What is the *only* variable that distinguishes you in the marketplace? Your people! The people who are operating those computers, working that equipment, and so on, are *the* link between process and profitability.

Start with your people, and the rest will follow much more easily. Customer loyalty is a direct result of a stable, trusting, and positive relationship with the people who sell to and service the customer. If I never see the same person twice when I visit your establishment, I lose confidence and comfort in doing business with you. But if I see Joe or Mary time after time, I start to feel connected and even obligated to respect the relationship, because I know that I will probably see this person again. I also know that this is a good organization if I see people sticking around.

Customers are more forgiving of our errors if they know and like us. If they know we have satisfied them before, and that our hearts are in the right place,

FIGURE I-1. THE CYCLE OF SATISFACTION.

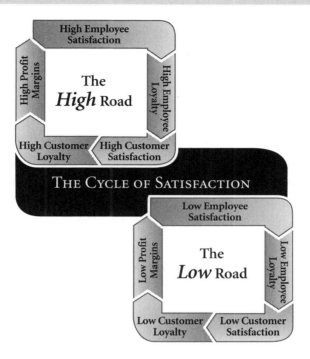

then they will be more understanding if and when we cannot hit a home run every time.

And finally, customers will even spend more money with us if they like us and trust us. If you tell me that I need something, and I know that you have never lied to me before, I will believe that you are looking out for my interests. If I don't know you and have never developed a positive relationship with you, then I will be leery of trusting your advice.

People + Process = Performance + Profitability

THE CYCLE OF EMPLOYMENT

When you completed the Human Resources Best Practices Self-Assessment at the beginning of this introduction, you were introduced to the Cycle of Employment, starting with your brand image as an employer and moving on to how and where you look for people, how you bring them on board, and so on.

Most organizations approach employment as a catch-as-catch-can process. We have a vacancy, so we place an ad or post a notice; we pray that people will call or stop in, then we interview those people (i.e., see if we like them) and ultimately hire the least of the evils and pray some more. How's this approach working for you?

The first step in the Cycle of Employment is your reputation, or brand image. One thing this kit cannot do for you is improve your image in the marketplace. However, if you follow the steps in this process, you *will* eventually make an impact on your reputation in the employment market and in the market in general. HR is PR! It cannot be overstated how critical your reputation is to your recruitment success. Great people gravitate to great employers.

Unfortunately, many businesses do a miserable job of public relations, particularly in the employment market. We do ourselves a serious disservice by not consciously creating a positive brand image of our company as a great place to work. We work so hard to create positive spin around our products, our services, or our mission, but we fail to see the direct correlation between our reputation as an employer and our success in the marketplace.

From now on, think about recruitment and HR overall as a public relations activity. Keep telling yourself that HR is PR! Pay attention to where you spend your time and money in the community. Rather than writing a check or sending volunteers for everything that comes down the pike, or at random, ask yourself if each activity is in alignment with your HR branding strategy.

Think about the message you send out when you interview, on-board, terminate, and carry out all the other HR activities in this kit that create positive or negative word of mouth in the community at large. People talk, and friends listen.

We aren't just in the market to sell our products or services. We are in the market to hire great people! In fact, if you look at the Cycle of Satisfaction, people come first. That's how you sell products and services, and that's how you create a positive brand image. We will talk about this in more detail in the "Creative Sourcing Strategies" section of Chapter 2.

In a nutshell, the Cycle of Employment (see Figure I-2) starts with your *reputation* (you can't hire someone who doesn't apply) and continues through the *recruitment* process and experience, after which you bring new employees on board (*reception*). From there, it is a function of how you *recognize* and *reward* performance, and you can hope that it continues until the employee's *retirement*. The overarching objective and result of all of this is *retention* (i.e., employee loyalty that leads to customer loyalty).

THE RECRUITMENT FUNNEL

As was mentioned in the HR Self-Assessment and the Cycle of Employment, recruitment does not begin when someone applies for a job. It begins with your reputation. Why do some organizations get the pick of the litter, while others have to settle for the losers? It's their reputation in the job market and in their communities.

FIGURE I-2. THE CYCLE OF EMPLOYMENT

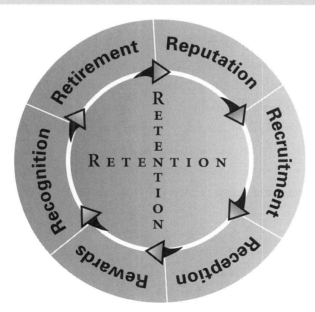

FIGURE I-3. THE RECRUITMENT FUNNEL: GARBAGE IN–GARBAGE OUT?

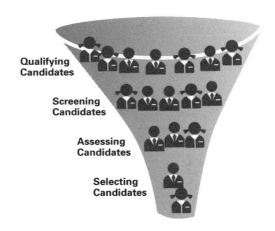

Qualifying Candidates

Screening Candidates

Assessing Candidates

Selecting Candidates

You can't hire someone who doesn't apply! If the best and the brightest aren't coming into the top of the funnel (see Figure I-3), then what do you expect to come out of the bottom? Garbage in? Garbage out!

Disney, Nordstrom, Southwest Airlines, Ritz-Carlton, and other such companies do not have nearly as much difficulty finding great people as other companies do; great people find them because they have great reputations. The good news for you is that you can have a more significant impact and footprint in your local community than any big organization can have nationally. You can be a bigger frog in a smaller pond.

Again, when you realize that recruitment is also public relations, you will start to look at your image in the marketplace more seriously. Look at where you spend your time, your money, and your effort in the community, and reengineer it to meet your recruitment objectives, not just your sales objectives.

PART **1**

PREEMPLOYMENT/RECRUITMENT

Recruiting used to be . . .

ONE INTERVIEW,
ONE WORK REFERENCE
MAYBE AN APPLICATION

... AND LOTS OF
"GUT INSTINCT!"

Now it's . . .

Assessing Risk

Drug Screen

Background Checks

Employee References

Qualifying the Applicant

Work Experience

Education & Training

Structured Interviews

Testing for Potential

Learning Aptitude

Behavioral Strengths
& Concerns

Performance Skills

CHAPTER 1

Preliminary Tools

WHY WORK HERE?

Most successful organizations can tell a prospective customer why that customer should buy from them, that is, their "Why Buy Here?" statement. Some call this a "UVP," or unique value proposition. This is what converts a product from a commodity (I can buy the same car anywhere from anybody at the same price) to a value-added, emotion-filled experience (I want to buy it from you). This is what creates both brand and company loyalty.

What most organizations fail to do, however, is to identify and define their "Why Work Here?" statement, which is what ultimately contributes the most to "Why Buy Here?". (See Figure I-1, "The Cycle of Satisfaction.")

Every shoe store has shoes. Every fast-food joint has burgers. Every airline has airplanes. It's the people who sell those shoes, who serve those burgers, and who work on those planes that create the unique experience, or UVP.

So, without the best and the brightest employees, performing at their peak, we are merely order takers offering a commodity, and we are dependent on luck rather than on a loyal, lucrative customer base. That's why we end up giving our products and services away, instead of selling value and improving our margins.

Recruitment is sales. Recruitment is PR. Every time you interview someone, you are sending a message about your organization, whether you hire that person or not. Why not make that message work for you?

The first step in accomplishing this is to have a well-defined "Why Work Here?"

statement that rolls off the tongue of anyone in the organization who is asked. It's your mantra. Here is how you can go about developing such a statement.

1. **Survey your long-term employees (if you have any).** Ask them the primary reason that they have been loyal to your organization. Ask them, "What's the best thing about working here?" (It may be a family atmosphere, great working conditions, recognition, fun, flexibility, and so on.)

2. **Document your history, culture, values, and any other characteristics** that make your organization different from, better than, or unique compared to your competition.

3. **Conduct a brainstorming session with your leadership team** to refine this information into a one- to two-sentence summation that anyone would be able to understand, and that would impress anyone who heard it. Try to boil it down to no more than three or four key concepts; otherwise, the intended message gets watered down.

Having worked with many organizations on this activity, we can tell you that it doesn't take months to accomplish this. Usually, if you ask enough people to define why someone would want to work for your company, you will start to see common themes and threads. That's exactly what you want to have happen, because then you know that the information you are getting is valid and pervasive.

For example, when we worked with a large chain of family restaurants, we surveyed the management team at its annual conference. In less than an hour, there were two things that came up over and over:

1. "Your opinion matters here."
2. "We have fun!"

Obviously that's not a lot of words, but it is certainly a great foundation on which to build. You can get quotes from employees, customers, and others to reinforce these key values and principles, which brings us to the next step in the Total HR process: the recruitment brochure. You will see some great "Why Work Here?" statements in the sample brochures in Figure 1-1 and on the CD.

THE RECRUITMENT BROCHURE

Once you have your "Why Work Here?" statement, you are ready to expand it to a recruitment brochure. Generally, these don't need to be anything more than a nice color trifold (and web page). But what goes into one?

Not that you need all of this, but here are some examples of what works well in a recruitment brochure:

- "Why Work Here?" statement
- Bird-dog referral bonus policy
- Employee photos and testimonials
- Key benefits
- Awards and accolades
- Pictures of your facility
- Web site address—directions to application form
- E-mail address for more information
- Map with directions to facility
- Name and phone number of primary contact for employment
- Equal opportunity statement

Since few, if any, organizations excel at this, you will be miles ahead of the competition if you have such a brochure. Figure 1-1 is an example of a very effective recruitment brochure. No matter what industry you are in, the principles are the same.

Notice that in Figure 1-1, the brochure from TrenchSafety and Supply, the company has five "Why Work Here?" statements:

1. "You'll Have a 'Say' in How We Do Things."
2. "You'll Make a Difference in the Community."
3. "You'll Enjoy Our Relaxed, Results-Oriented Atmosphere."
4. "You'll Appreciate Our 'Open-Book' Management."
5. "You'll Receive Excellent Compensation and Benefits."

FIGURE 1-1. TRENCHSAFETY AND SUPPLY RECRUITING BROCHURE

The two workers in these TrenchSafety-supplied trench boxes on an Arkansas job site went home to their families at the end of their workday. Without those boxes, they would have gone somewhere else.

*How About
5 Great Reasons
to Work at
TrenchSafety...*

TRENCH**SAFETY**™
AND SUPPLY, INC.
Memphis, Tennessee • 901/346-5800 • 800/865-5801 • FAX 901/346-1060
North Little Rock, Arkansas • 501/955-3800 • 800/243-6408 • FAX 501/955-2044
www.TrenchSafety.com

TRENCH**SAFETY**™
AND SUPPLY, INC.
Memphis, Tennessee
North Little Rock, Arkansas

www.TrenchSafety.com

OK, 6 GREAT REASONS

1. You'll Have a 'Say' in How We Do Things

Trench Safety is a small company. And that is by design. We like it that way. Because by staying small, each employee's contribution makes a difference. ■ Do you see a better way to process an order? Speak up. Know of a new product that might help our customers do their jobs better? Or save them money? Bring your ideas to the table. Heard about a way we might be able to save some money? ■ Let's see if it'll work at TrenchSafety.

2. You'll Make a Difference in the Community

TrenchSafety is unique. Few companies offer the products and services we do. And fewer still provide the high level of service that we deliver every day. ■ We help build and maintain the infrastructure in our communities — the water, sewer, gas, electrical, telecommunications, and highway systems. It is difficult to drive around the Mid-South and **not** see the impact of TrenchSafety. ■ And, the products and services we provide save lives. Construction and utility work can be very dangerous, particularly when workers aren't properly trained, and don't use their equipment correctly. ■ TrenchSafety is recognized as the Mid-South leader in construction-industry safety training. More than 6,500 people have been through our safety courses. In fact, many referrals to our training classes come from OSHA personnel.

3. You'll Enjoy Our Relaxed, Results-Oriented Atmosphere

No coats and ties here. No dress codes. We expect our employees to be neat, and dress appropriately. But we're not a bank or big-city law firm. ■ We also

strive to make our work fun and enjoyable. If you're not happy where you spend the better part of your day, we both have a problem. ■ By the same token, we've all got a job to do. We provide first-rate service to our customers. We respect our fellow employees. We're good neighbors in the community. Of course, we're in business to make a profit, and this work enviroment enables us to do so.

4. You'll Appreciate Our "Open Book" Management

Imagine going to a football game where they didn't tell you the score. It wouldn't be a lot of fun to watch. A lot of businesses are run that way. The people in such companies don't know how the business is doing. ■ At TrenchSafety we practice "open-book" management. What does that mean to you? It means we openly and frequently discuss our financial results…with everyone on the team. The end-result is that we all do a better job when we know the score. And we make more money for ourselves and for the company.

5. You'll Receive Excellent Compensation & Benefits

TrenchSafety provides fair and competitive compensation programs. To attract and retain top talent, we know we have to pay accordingly. ■ Though always subject to change, we also offer health insurance, life and disability insurance, sick pay, paid vacation time, and a 401K retirement plan that includes an attractive employer-matching provision. ■ We also offer, on a regular basis, incentive programs tied to financial and other objectives. Such incentives are always over

and above other compensation programs. Some of these programs have lasted for just a month or two. Others have lasted six months or longer.

6. You'll Value Your Opportunities for Advancement

TrenchSafety provides a winning combination of products and services, and that combination means we plan to grow. As you help in that effort, you'll have terrific opportunities to advance. ■ A great example is our Branch Manager in Memphis. In 1998 he began working at TrenchSafety as our laser and machine-control technician. Today he's running the location.

Let's Talk About the Possibilities

To be sure, you'll work hard, you'll enjoy a great working environment and benefits, and you'll build a solid future. ■ If a career at TrenchSafety sounds interesting to you, or if you know of someone who might be interested, contact us today!

800/865-5801
901/346-5800
901/346-1060 FAX
careers@TrenchSafety.com

For organizations that do not produce or sell a product, the "Why Work Here?" statement is different. For example, the Montana Department of Environmental Quality's statement is "Be a Part of Something Big"—specifically, "working for a clean and healthful environment" (see recruitment brochure on the CD).

Also on the CD is the U.S. Consumer Product Safety Commission's brochure, which emphasizes more tangible reasons, such as their benefits package, flexible work schedules, and so on. And its mission is also a great "Why Work Here?" statement: "Saving Lives and Keeping Families Safe."

As mentioned, this kit is supposed to be a step-by-step building process. Once you have perfected your recruitment brochure, it's a snap to post it on your organization's web site as a recruitment tool. We will talk more about that in "Creative Sourcing Strategies" in Chapter 2.

JOB DESCRIPTIONS (AKA "SUCCESS PROFILES")

Why have job descriptions? Some things may be obvious, but let us count the ways:

1. They force you to focus and come to a consensus about what the job is.
2. They help you identify the skills, traits, and other requirements for the job.
3. They help you keep your objectivity and consistency when assessing candidates.
4. They clarify for job candidates whether the job is something that they can or want to do.
5. They are the basis for orientation and performance management.
6. They provide the foundation for career paths and succession planning.
7. They can protect you from certain legal claims, such as disability charges.
8. They can be used to determine the competitiveness of your compensation.

What follows are a couple of different examples of job descriptions. The components are the same no matter what the job may be, so you can go to the CD, select the template that best suits your needs, and fill in the blanks for your own positions. If a particular section is not applicable for some reason, just delete it or insert N/A. This way, one form fits all.

Please be sure to clearly communicate the good, the bad, and the ugly of the job, as this is a form of insurance to prevent problems later on. It is better to have someone realize that he is not a good fit for the job *before* you hire him rather than after. This is called self-selection or self-screening. In HR terms, it is called a realistic job preview.

In our experience with clients over the years, there are always some who are fearful of having job descriptions because they do not want an employee saying, "That's not in my job description." This is easily overcome, as you can see in the "Duties and Responsibilities" section, by adding the phrase "Other duties may be assigned."

It is better to have job descriptions that provide some guidance and expectations than to have nothing, and have to manage by default. It is not expected that you will include every single detail of the job in every job description, but it is also unrealistic to think that you can manage someone's performance if everyone is not operating from a common understanding of what the job requires. By providing this, you're already helping the employee pave her personal road to success with your company.

Thus, a job description should be viewed as much more than just a description of the job—it's a definition of what it will take to be successful in that role for your company. That's why we prefer to call them "success profiles" instead of "job descriptions." Words matter! Here is a comparison. You choose!

JOB DESCRIPTION

Job Title: Customer Service Representative
Department: Sales
Reports To: Customer Service Manager
FLSA Status:
Prepared By:
Prepared Date:
Revision Date:

SUMMARY

Processes orders for merchandise received by mail, telephone, fax, or e-mail, or personally from a customer or organization employee, by performing the following duties.

ESSENTIAL DUTIES AND RESPONSIBILITIES include the following. Other duties may be assigned.

Edits orders received for price and nomenclature.

Informs customer of unit prices, shipping date, anticipated delays, and any additional information needed by customer.

Advises customer if the order is close to the current dollar discount and inquires if customer would like to take advantage of the discount by adding to the order.

Writes or types order form, or enters data into computer, to determine total cost for customer.

Prints shipment documents and forwards to the Customer Service Manager for review.

Records or files copy of orders received.

Follows up on orders to ensure delivery by specified dates.

Computes price, discount, sales representative's commission, and shipping charges as required.

Prepares invoices and shipping documents such as export papers and commercial invoices.

Checks shipping orders to ensure that they are accurate with regard to quantity shipped; this is done by comparing shipping documents with computer-generated reports.

Specifies if special labeling is required for shipment and in some instances supplies such labeling to the shipping department.

Receives and checks into customer complaints.

Confers with production, shipping, warehouse, or common carrier personnel to expedite or trace missing or delayed shipments.

Compiles statistics and prepares various reports for management.

Answers questions from customers or individuals on how a product operates or directs them to the person who is able to assist them.

Makes sure that quotes are processed through the quoting process in a timely manner.

Types quotes and maintains files for all quotes that are processed.

Maintains customer name and address database.

Responsible for sending new pricing, with the correct multiplier, to all customers.

Creates no charge shippers for customer replacements.

QUALIFICATIONS

To perform this job successfully, an individual must be able to perform each essential duty satisfactorily. The requirements listed here are representative of the knowledge, skill, and/or ability required. Reasonable accommodations may be made to enable individuals with disabilities to perform the essential functions.

EDUCATION AND/OR EXPERIENCE

High school diploma or general education degree (GED); or one to three months related experience and/or training; or equivalent combination of education and experience.

LANGUAGE SKILLS

Ability to read and interpret documents such as procedure manuals, work instructions, and software manuals. Ability to write routine reports and correspondence. Ability to speak and communicate well with customers.

MATHEMATICAL SKILLS

Ability to add, subtract, multiply, and divide in all units of measure, using whole numbers, common fractions, and decimals.

REASONING ABILITY

Ability to apply commonsense understanding to carry out instructions furnished in written, oral, or diagram form. Ability to deal with problems involving several concrete variables in standardized situations.

OTHER SKILLS AND ABILITIES

Must be familiar with current software packages such as Microsoft Word and Excel.

Must be familiar with all product lines and customer base.

Must be familiar with the data works system and be able to input and retrieve data.

CERTIFICATES, LICENSES, REGISTRATIONS

None required for this position.

PHYSICAL DEMANDS The physical demands described here are representative of those that must be met by an employee to successfully perform the essential functions of this job. Reasonable accommodations may be made to enable individuals with disabilities to perform the essential functions.

Individuals may need to sit or stand as needed. May require walking primarily on a level surface for periodic periods throughout the day. Reaching above shoulder heights or below the waist or lifting as required to file documents or store materials throughout the workday. Proper lifting techniques required. May include lifting up to 25 pounds for files or computer printouts on occasion.

WORK ENVIRONMENT The work environment characteristics described here are representative of those that an employee encounters while performing the essential functions of this job. Reasonable accommodations may be made to enable individuals with disabilities to perform the essential functions.

The performance of this position may occasionally require exposure to the manufacturing areas where certain areas require the use of personal protective equipment such as safety glasses with side shields and mandatory hearing protection.

For the most part, ambient room temperatures, lighting, and traditional office equipment as found in a typical office environment.

Success Profile—Consultant

Position Title: Consultant		Reports to:	
Department or Job Family:		Approved by:	
Date Modified:		Modified by:	
Compensation Strategy: $60k–$145k		FSLA Status:	

ABOUT (YOUR COMPANY):

_____ was founded in 19___ by IT professionals who recognized a need for quality IT infrastructure and operations management technologies, best practices in process and implementation, and specialists expert in their design, implementation, and use. Recently listed as one of the *Inc.* 500 fastest-growing privately held companies, _____ helps IT organizations extend their service capabilities.

PURPOSE/MISSION:

_____ is seeking candidates interested in accelerating their career by implementing numerous software solutions. Service Management and Systems software is utilized to manage and monitor information technology infrastructure around the world. From project management, software development life cycle, release to production, asset management, quality assurance and performance, to infrastructure monitoring, performance, and maintenance, XYZ software runs information technology and requires knowledgeable, talented consultants to guide customers through the implementation process to realize the software's full potential.

PRIMARY RESPONSIBILITIES:

- Develop custom integrations using programming skills.
- System integration skills required to create monitoring and intersystem exchange of information.
- Collaborate with local application development teams using middleware that includes Oracle, Sybase, Weblogic, MQSeries, Tibco, etc.
- Log records of change and incidents to comply with various industry and government standards.
- Lead the IT organization through the changes needed in order to make use of the enterprise systems management/business service management tools.
- Travel extensively and handle your own travel.
- Responsible for SOW—handoff and handback process.
- Responsible for creating 60-plus-page technical documents and weekly status reporting.
- Make presentations.

PERFORMANCE SKILLS:

- Communication
- Conflict management
- Commitment to task
- Customer focus
- Energizing others

- Systematic problem solving
- Decision making and problem solving
- Planning, prioritizing, and goal setting
- Policies, processes, and procedures
- Teamwork

EDUCATION/EXPERIENCE REQUIREMENTS:

- BS in computer science or computer-related major

TECHNICAL EXPERIENCE:

- Minimum 5 years experience with various XYZ software and/or associated products

Platform-Specific (examples)	Other Vendors (examples)
BAC—Business Availability Center	CiscoWorks—Cisco Systems
SiteScopen	Genious—NetScout
MAM—Application Mapper	Nagious—Open Source
EUM—End User Manager	Big Brother
RUM—Real User Manager	MRTG
NNM—Network Node Manager	Netcool
OVOW—Operations Center Windows	Openview Advanced Access
OVOU—Operations Center Unix	Nastel
Many Various Openview Smart Plug-ins	BladeLogic
Performance Insight/Manager/Reporter	Oracle Grid Control

Opsware

Mercury Performance Center 8.1

VuGen

Mercury Quality Center

Quick Test Professional

Mercury Dashboard

Mercury Kitana/PVCS/ITG/PPM

Managed Technologies

Oracle/DB2/Sybase/SQL Server

Weblogic/Websphere/ATG Dynamo

PeopleSoft/SAP/Yantra

Apache/IIS/iPlanet

JBoss/JRun/JRocket/Tomcat

Control-M/Meastro/Autosys

Tibco/MQ Series

Veritas Cluster Server/Sun Cluster/
    MC ServiceGuard

Veritas Filesystem/Volume
    Manager/Solaris Disksuite

Netbackup

Remedy

TOAD

Microsoft Office Suite

Visio

Microsoft Project

Exceed

Internet Information Server (IIS)

Programming Languages

Perl

C/C++

Shell (csh/ksh/bash)

Mongrel Ruby on Rails

Phython

XML/HTML/XHTML

Java/JSP

Perforce/CVS/SVN

PL/SQL

INDUSTRY EXPERIENCE:

➤ Minimum of 7 years of industry experience

➤ Consulting project experience with the proposal, specification, design, implementation, and support of systems and service software–oriented projects.

➤ Minimum of 3 years of experience in the day-to-day issues of administering a corporate network and systems environment.

➤ In-depth knowledge of network and systems administration and system performance.

➤ In-depth knowledge of TCP/IP, SNMP, and other networking standards (e.g., Novell IPX, ATM, frame relay).

➤ Strong programming skills a necessity.

➤ Hands-on experience with network routers, hubs, and switches, including configuration and troubleshooting.

➤ Knowledgeable in Internet infrastructure requirements, including firewalls and basic security practices.

➤ Strong desire to continue to increase technical knowledge.

➤ Strong communication skills—oral and written. Must be able to serve as the lead author for large technical documents.

CERTIFICATIONS:

Other Certifications

➤   ITIL Foundations Certification
➤   Black/Green Belt Six Sigma

GOALS:

_____

_____

CHAPTER 2

Recruitment

CREATIVE SOURCING STRATEGIES

We do not recommend that you embark on a lot of these creative recruitment strategies until you have implemented some of the other key initiatives in the kit (the "Why Work Here?" statement, the recruitment brochure, the web site, success profiles, and so on). However, you should be thinking about which ones you will use when you are ready to improve the quality and quantity of your candidates.

Remember the recruitment funnel? (See Figure I-3.) Even if we have better candidates coming into the top of the funnel, it would be in vain if we didn't do a better job of screening, selection, on-boarding, and so on, so that we have the best candidates coming out of the bottom of the funnel. And then we have to keep them on board and keep them performing. We don't want to open the floodgates before we're ready to handle the flow.

Before we get into the more creative and productive sourcing methods, it is important to understand two key principles about recruiting, and how the best organizations approach it.

Active versus Passive Candidates

People who are responding to job postings or ads to look for a job are what we call *active* candidates; that is, they are actively looking for work. There is nothing wrong with that, but you are missing out on the rest of the population, especially those who are already gainfully and successfully employed. Just because they are employed doesn't mean that they are happy where they are or that they wouldn't be interested in working for you (especially if you are doing everything we are recommending in this kit!).

Superstars generally are not studying employment ads and job boards. Nor are they listed on Internet job boards. They don't need to be. If you want to hire the best of the best of your industry, you have to go to them, which means that you must identify and search for *passive* candidates.

And the best way to do that, besides just calling people and asking them if they would like to come to work for you, is to understand the next principle.

Intensive versus Continuous Recruitment

The other shift in thinking that is necessary is to change *when* you recruit. If you wait until you have a vacancy to start looking for candidates, you are engaged in *intensive* recruiting. In other words, you have to scurry and blitz to get candidates into the pipeline, and then you are forced to settle for whomever you can find at the moment. Time is not on your side.

A better and actually easier approach is to be recruiting every day, everywhere you are. Whether you are at church, a restaurant, the grocery store, or somewhere else, your antennae should always be up and running. It's called the Law of Attraction. What you think about becomes more visible to you.

Have you ever been thinking about a new car? Have you noticed that when you are thinking about a particular model, you suddenly start seeing more and more cars of that model on the road? It's an awareness that creates a new focus. The same principle works for recruitment.

This leads us to the concept of transferable skills. Quit looking where everyone else looks. Just because a guy sold widgets in the past doesn't mean that he's the best and brightest candidate to sell widgets for you, or for anyone else, for that matter.

You may find a great waiter who really understands customer satisfaction and handling skills, long and tough hours and conditions, and so on, which makes him a perfect candidate who has the style and the skills to succeed in your industry or environment. The concept here is to hire candidates based on what they can be, as opposed to what they have been.

Cards for Everyone!

Get business cards for your entire staff. Not only are they an ego booster and motivator (especially for those who have never had a business card), but they turn everyone in your organization into an ambassador. What's one of the first questions people ask each other when they meet? It's "What do you do?" And in our society, that means "Where do you work?" What a powerful "Why Work Here?" statement it is for everyone to be able to say, "I work at _____" and then hand over a business card.

And on the back, put a statement to the effect that "we are always looking for great people!" and advertise your bird-dog incentive (see the next idea).

Bird Dogs for Everyone!

One of the highest-quality and lowest-cost sources of great people is referrals. Many organizations pay an incentive (aka bird-dog bonus) if an employee refers someone who buys its product or service. That's smart. But, here's something even smarter: Pay people who refer someone who becomes an employee!

Advertise wherever you can that you will pay for great people. That's why we said to put it on the back of all the business cards you are going to get printed. But tell your vendors, suppliers, service providers, and anyone else you trust who could refer good people.

This doesn't mean that you are going to hire everyone. It only means that you are going to have a larger pool of higher-quality candidates from which to choose coming into the top of the funnel. Most people will not refer someone who is going to make them look bad, so there is an automatic upgrade in the quality of the pool of candidates from this source.

One last suggestion: Pay half of the bonus on the date of hire, and the other half six months down the road. This way, you don't pay the whole thing if the person doesn't stay long enough to return your investment. You are rewarding both recruitment and retention. That's return on investment (ROI)!

A complete sample Employee Referral Program follows at the end of this section, and can also be found on the enclosed CD.

Boomerangs

The two most lucrative sources of candidates are bird dogs (referrals) and boomerangs (returnees). Ironically, one of the sources that companies overlook the most is their own alumni. Because of the power and importance of this source, it deserves a lot more detail and strategy. You can pick and choose which of the following strategies will work best for you.

It is amazing that there are still employers out there who would never consider "letting" someone who had left "the organization" come back. Who are you punishing? If that same person applied for a job with your organization, but had *not* worked for you before, would you hire her? If so, that means that it is better *not* to have a track record with your organization. Duuh?

Face it, if you hire the best and the brightest, it stands to reason that those people will be the hardest to hold onto. Anyone can hold onto a loser. If you have very low turnover, before you break your arm patting yourself on the back, be sure that it isn't because you have people that no one else wants or people who have no other options.

If you know for a fact that you would rehire a particular ex-employee (for example, if he has a rare talent, you know it, and you'll always need it), give him a "Get Out of Jail Free" card that entitles him to immediate reemployment without having to go through Human Resources or any other bureaucratic process requirements.

"You want a job? You got it!" This is a powerful symbolic gesture that reinforces an employee's value to you and leaves him with a very positive last (and lasting) impression of what he is leaving. He can escape the jail of your competition at any time.

Human Resources people often bristle at such an idea, and are quick to ask, "What about references and background checks, and all the other preliminary work that has to be done?" Why do you need to check references or complete any other preemployment requirements for such people? You've already hired them once, and they obviously proved themselves or you wouldn't want them back, right? You've already got something better than references or credentials; you've got past performance.

If it is really necessary, make the hiring offer contingent upon whatever security blankets you need, but you surely don't need to go back beyond the date you hired the person before! Not only is that a waste of time and money, but it sure doesn't say much for your process the first time around.

Just be sure to make it clear on the "Get Out of Jail Free" card that the offer is contingent upon a suitable position being available and that current employees have first priority.

There are other benefits to rehiring former employees as well. They can come in running, they know the culture and fit into it, they do not need an orientation to your policies and procedures, they know the people and the processes, *and* they have fresh ideas and perspectives that come from having been outside of your box for a while. Need we go on? OK, we will.

When a high performer leaves, don't let your ego get in the way of your success as an employer. Show regret, wish the person well, and tell her that you would love to have her back if the new employment situation doesn't work out the way she hopes it will.

Next, to capitalize on the fact that the honeymoon period always ends, tell these high performers that if they return to your organization within one year, you will not only restore their prior service, but also "bridge" their service for the time they were gone (i.e., they will be treated as if they had never left).

This means that their vacation schedule is reinstated and any other perks of tenure continue to build as if they had never left you. Datatel (a software solutions organization based in Fairfax, Virginia) is a perfect case in point. It warmly refers to its rehires as "retreads" and gives full credit for prior service toward what it calls "time-based benefits" *regardless* of how long ago they terminated.

Think about this. It costs nothing if these people do not exercise the option, and next to nothing if they do, but it plants a seed in their brains that for the next year, they can defect from your competition and be kept whole by coming back to you. They can have their cake and eat it, too.

If you have to justify it another way, think of such people as having been on a leave of absence or a sabbatical. The ROI on this incentive is huge if you recover valuable talent. The bottom line is, employees who leave and come back are the most loyal employees you will ever have.

There are several other twists that you can put on this incentive. For example, what if the first year passes and you still want to lure someone back? You can offer to restore but not bridge the person's service. Or, you can add the caveat that this bridge or restoration of service will not take effect until the person has been back with you for at least another year. Don't just reward returning; reward retention as well.

You can design the parameters any way you want. Just be sure that you apply the criteria consistently and legally. Again, this is a very inexpensive yet effective way of keeping your hooks in former employees for as long as possible, to start realizing a return on your prior investment, to steal them back from the competition, and to maximize retention, all at the same time.

Just as colleges use alumni associations to keep in touch and keep people contributing, your organization can do the same. It's not a sign of failure to have a lot of ex-employees. It may even be a sign of success: Your graduates are in demand! The only problem is that you paid for their tuition. Don't you want to recoup your investment?

Create a database of alumni and keep in touch with them, both electronically and by hard copy. Invite them to appropriate organization events (announcements, annual meetings, picnics, and so on). Send them your newsletter, press releases, and other positive communications so that they not only remember that you exist, but see that you are doing well, even without them. Again, treat them as if they were on leave or on sabbatical. They're not dead!

Booz Allen Hamilton really put some muscle behind its alumni efforts. It actually created a position called manager of alumni programs and made that person responsible for managing the database (over 3,000 alumni) and coordinating the publishing of an alumni directory. The directory, which goes to all alumni, lists names alphabetically, the year the person left the firm, and cross-references for geography and even former surnames. Bain & Co., a Boston-based international consulting firm, has more people in its alumni association than it has on its payroll!

Even better, personalize this process. Assign your alumni to various "linkages" (i.e., current employees) within the organization who will manage the relationship and keep in touch in other ways. They can attach personal notes to your alumni mailings, or even call them or meet with them on occasion. You can even create an incentive for the linkage people in the event that one of their alums returns to the fold (see "Bird Dogs for Everyone").

A trickle-down benefit from maintaining good relationships with former employees is that they will continue to speak well of you. Remember, recruitment is PR and should be continuous. In-Focus Systems, Inc., a manufacturer of computer projectors based in Wilsonville, Oregon, is a good case in point. As a result of its alumni program, it gets referrals from former employees all the time. People will call and say that they just interviewed so and so, and she was really good, but they did not have the right position for her, so they are referring her to you.

One last suggestion: Be sure to get an e-mail address for people when they leave, and preferably not their work address, but rather their personal e-mail address at home. This is a very effective way to stay in touch with large numbers of people after they leave. It's quick and nonintrusive.

Leaving your organization should not be viewed as a betrayal. It is natural for valuable talent to pursue new opportunities. Remember, your best people are the ones who are most likely to leave, because they are the best people. Get them back!

One of our clients even rehired an average employee just so that others in the firm could see that the grass isn't always greener on the other side of the fence. This is another major side benefit to hiring boomerangs: It tells your current staff that yours is a better place to work.

If you have an internal job-posting process, why not put your alumni on the distribution list? The placement office is just another benefit of having graduated from your organization. To avoid offending your current employees, alumni can go into a second-tier priority status.

In other words, for positions that are not filled by current employees, your alumni get preference over the rest of the world. Not only does that dangle another carrot in front of potentially disenchanted alums, but it is also a whole lot cheaper and more reliable than using headhunters or traditional advertising.

Forrester Research, Inc., of Cambridge, Massachusetts, is a good example of this concept. In fact, Forrester built a web site and a common network where it posts jobs and offers a referral bonus to former employees who refer candidates that get hired. Forrester anticipates that some of the former employees will be attracted to the current jobs and will throw their own hats into the ring.

So, let's say that one of these boomerang strategies works. An alumnus has come back! This is cause for celebration, so take advantage of the opportunity to showcase your success. Rehiring a former employee is a great excuse for showing off, both internally and externally.

Send out publicity and press releases to both your local media and the media in the alum's hometown, college press, and other such places. After all, that's where you found this person. What a great testimonial to you as an employer—people who leave actually come back. And don't forget to send a copy of the homecoming invitation to your boomerangs-to-be. Get them thinking, too!

Have a party. Get a decorated cake, confetti, the whole thing. After all, look at all the money you saved by not paying for ads or an agency, and not hiring an unknown. Oh, and by the way, be sure that one of the welcome back gifts is an engraved boomerang.

Vendors

Your vendors are indebted to you. So, they should want to please you. How about the UPS driver? Or the janitorial service? Or the coffee vendor? Can you imagine how many people these people see every week? If one of them thought that he could earn a couple of extra bucks on the side by referring candidates, he would jump at the opportunity. Give them your card or recruitment brochure with your bird-dog bonus program on it.

This goes for anyone who walks through your door to sell you something. It's ROI time again!

Your Web Site

Look at your web site from the perspective of a recruiting tool, not just a sales tool. Can viewers easily see an application link on your home page? Can they take a virtual tour of your facility? Is your "Why Work Here?" statement clearly identifiable? Is your recruitment brochure on your site? Every page should have a link button to your electronic application for employment.

You've already got a web site, so make it work for you.

Newspaper Ads

If you are relying on the classified ads in your local newspaper to find job candidates, you might as well just use the money and the newspaper to start a fire. Stop it! Not that we want to put the newspaper industry out of business, but it is going in that direction on its own anyway. And you'll never recruit young people through the newspaper. What the heck is a newspaper?

As you should know by now, this is not the best place to put your hard-earned money. However, if you must, then run an ad somewhere outside the classifieds, in a section that your potential recruits would be reading, such as the sports section or the lifestyle section. This way, your ad isn't swimming in the sea of other "help wanted" ads, and you are more likely to attract a passive candidate. But generally speaking, unless you are looking for retirees to be greeters at Wal-Mart, don't waste your money here.

Trade Publications

A more cost-effective and targeted use of advertising dollars is in niche publications. From the local horse trader or penny saver to club and association newsletters and any other trade or special-interest publication, you can stand out from the crowd, and spend a lot less money and get a much larger ad. Figure out what your target market reads, and advertise there. It's cheaper, more focused, and not lost in a sea of other ads.

Vocational and Trade Schools

Start building relationships with your local vocational and trade schools. Remember, recruitment is public relations. Also, you can get in front of potential candidates on their turf, and educate and enlighten them on your organization.

Also, when you have developed a strong relationship with the faculty, they will tell you who their best candidates are because they want their students to get jobs, and they want you to continue hiring those students. It's a win-win, and it costs next to nothing.

High School Career Days

The same principle that applies to vocational and trade schools also applies to general public and parochial high schools. Go to their career days; invite them for an insider tour/showcase of your business. Sponsor a contest. Just get creative.

Many companies really need to do a better job of "educating" the public on the virtues and positives of working in their industry or profession.

Job Fairs and Conventions

Although job fairs are a great one-stop-shop for seeing a lot of people all at once, they are kind of in the same category as running a classified ad. Again, you are lost in a sea of people and other employers. Unless you can do something to really stand out, there are better places to spend your time and money. Job fairs are fine to keep your name and image out there, but don't expect tons of superstars to be crossing your path. It's a *crap* shoot.

Moonlighters/Hobbyists

Not all employees need to be career or full-time employees. There may be gearheads out there who would just like to "dabble" in the car business or hone their craft. There may be amateur chefs who would like to work part time assisting in a kitchen. There may be schoolteachers who want to tutor in the summer.

Find people who have a love for your industry or your product or service, or who have a love of sales, and let them build their own job. You probably won't have to provide benefits, and if you put them on incentive, you pay only for what they produce. There's little to lose and lots to gain. And, they're there because they *want* to be, not just because it's a job!

Retired/Older Workers

More and more people are working well into their golden years—many because they lack the gold to retire, and others because they are just bored. Either way, seniors can make excellent employees. If they're good enough for Wal-Mart or McDonald's, they should be good enough for you.

Find where seniors congregate (McDonald's at 7:00 A.M.; the senior center; the bank on the first of the month) and start working the crowd. Tell them what you have to offer, and see what happens. Give them two copies of your business card with the referral information on it, one for them and one for a friend. Even if they don't apply, they can still earn that bird-dog bonus.

Retiring/Exiting Military Personnel

Like retired or older workers, ex-military personnel make especially attractive candidates. Many times, they are drawing lifetime benefits already, and they have great skills, grooming, and discipline.

When I was working for J.D. Power & Associates, I remember evaluating a big Ford dealership in a beach resort town where the general manager was a retired admiral from the U.S. Navy. Not only did he run a tight ship (the dealership got perfect scores every year), but Ford got someone who was hugely overqualified because he could live and work in a resort setting, pull down some decent bucks, do it while also collecting a military pension, and do it with ease.

Talk about a win-win!

Competitors

Actually, we probably do a little too much of this in some businesses. Many of the people we hire are retreads from down the road who have been around the block several times. There's nothing inherently wrong with this, but some retreads are dangerous.

If you are going to steal from your competitors, steal their winners. Find out who won the consultant of the year award, or who is the world-class analyst. These are the passive candidates we referred to earlier. Just because they are not actively looking for a job doesn't mean that you can't appeal to their ego and their wallet. Polish off your "Why Work Here?" statement, and go get 'em!

This is another place where your own people can pitch in. If you are at the top of your game, in whatever profession it is, you should know who the movers and shakers are. You should be attending professional meetings, conferences, symposiums, and other such events, and seeing who is getting published in the journals, getting the recognition and awards, and making waves in the industry or profession. Connect with them and then go after them!

Employment Agencies (Contingency versus Retainer)

We are not staunch advocates of using employment agencies in most situations. For the money, you can do better for yourself, unless you are just lazy, have deep pockets, and would rather just farm it out.

Just FYI, there are basically two types of agencies. A contingency agency does not get paid a commission until the job is filled, and then it gets a percentage of the first year's annual compensation. A retainer agency gets paid up front, along with travel and other expenses, and is usually used only for high-level executives or hard-to-find skill sets.

New Hires

We have no qualms about asking new customers for referrals, so why not ask new employees for candidate referrals?

At the time of hire, ask your new recruits if they know of anyone who might want to come to work for you. Think about their attitude on their first day or week on the job. They want to please you. They are untainted, and winners tend to hang with other winners, so if you hire winners, leverage them.

Again, advise them of your bird-dog bonus program, and encourage them to take advantage of it.

Other Industries (Transferable Skills)

There are tons of high-performing workers out there in other industries who are ideal transplants into your industry. You don't necessarily need someone who has sold your product or service before. You need someone who can sell, *period*!

For example, furloughed flight attendants are a possible target market. They understand weird hours, tough conditions, and difficult customers. Workers from the hospitality industry (hotels, restaurants, and casinos) also have similar transferable skills. Look for attitude and work ethic. The rest can be trained.

Bankruptcies, Shutdowns, Cutbacks

In every crisis there is an opportunity! Pick up a copy of your local business newspaper (go to www.bizjournals.com) and go to the back pages, where all the fine print is that few people read. This is a gold mine!

There will be bankruptcies, judgments, liens, mortgages, and all sorts of information about what is happening in your own economic backyard. If you see that an organization in your community has filed for Chapter 7 bankruptcy, it is going down. This is not a reorganization, like Chapter 11. The firm is closing its doors.

Not only can you find great people who weren't looking for a job until now, but you can be a community hero by opening your doors to displaced workers in search of new employment. This is another great opportunity to use recruitment as a public relations and community relations activity, and an opportunity to find previously passive candidates as well.

Call the CEO or other top official, tell her that you are sorry to see that the organization is experiencing bad times, and then tell her that you will do whatever you can to help her out. Tell her the types of jobs you have and the skills that you need (job descriptions), and maybe even set up a career day dedicated to that organization.

Internet Job Boards

Internet job boards are the modern-day equivalent of the old classified ads, but much cheaper and better. If you haven't tried them, we recommend that you do so.

Even better, go to an industry-specific job board. Just do an Internet keyword search for the specific position and put the words "job board" in the search engine.

While you are at it, consider going outside your immediate market area if you find outstanding candidates. We know that you don't normally recruit front-line staff and other such employees from across the country, but why not? The wider the net you cast, the bigger the fish you can catch. The best and brightest talent is not always living in your backyard.

Offer to pay relocation expenses, contingent upon a year of continuous employment. In other words, it's a loan until they repay it with their service. It's also a retention tool, so that you can get your ROI.

Jailbirds (Ex-Cons)

Have you lost your mind? We know that's what you are probably thinking right now. Perhaps we have, but that has nothing to do with this idea. Granted, this requires some judiciousness. You shouldn't hire a bank robber to manage your accounting department, but there are lots of first-time offenders, bad luck bears, and others who realize that this is their last chance to make something of themselves.

Trust us; we have spoken with quite a few organizations that have gone this route, and more times than not, they have landed a great and loyal worker. Remember, the employee will have a parole or probation officer breathing down his neck, so chances are, if you make the right job-person match, it could be a win-win. Just arrange a meeting with the warden and discuss the possibilities.

Remember, transferable skills! (PS: Do not share the person's background with anyone who doesn't have a *need* to know.)

Your Employment Application

Just as you should ask your new hires for referrals, you can also ask those who haven't even been hired yet. Put a statement about your bird-dog bonus program at the end of your application form, and see what happens.

You may not have the perfect position for the person who is applying, but she can still make a couple of bucks by referring friends or relatives for jobs that may be a fit for someone else.

Your Own Candidate Files (Continuous versus Intensive Recruiting)

If you maintain the good employment records that we will be preaching about later in the kit (candidate folders, for example) and keep them organized by position and date, you can eventually mine your own database when a job vacancy occurs. That's when you move from intensive recruitment to continuous recruitment.

You may have interviewed someone a year ago, but you didn't hire him because he chose to go elsewhere, or it wasn't a perfect match at the time, but things change. Maybe this person isn't happy where he is, or maybe the position you are looking to fill now is a better fit, but whatever you do, keep good records, and keep going back to them. It's free!

EMPLOYEE REFERRAL PROGRAMS (aka BIRD DOGS)

As was suggested earlier, employee referral programs can be one of the most powerful recruiting tools. They have been proven to produce the highest volume of high-quality hires and have been statistically proven to lower your rates of attrition.

In fact, it has also been proven that your boomerang employees will be more loyal and dedicated than those who have never left and come back. They will have a higher level of commitment to you and your organization, and maybe even a little healthy guilt.

As this is one of the most powerful of the creative sourcing strategies, we thought it would be valuable to expand on this process and provide some sample guidelines that you can tailor to your own organization.

When thoughtfully designed, an employee referral program can be cost-effective and produce one of the highest ROIs of all of the HR focus areas. Well-designed programs can easily produce the majority of hires, with some firms getting more than 75 percent of their hires through such a program.

Employee Referral Bonus Program (Sample)

The appropriate personnel must approve the Employee Referral Bonus Program before it is implemented. The bonus amounts must be approved before any bonuses are granted. The following are general guidelines for implementing an Employee Referral Program.

Eligibility. All regular **(Company Name)** employees are eligible to earn a referral bonus with the exception of HR department employees, directors, VP-level employees, and the hiring manager or supervisor.

Referrals must be registered with the HR department at the beginning of the prospective employee interview in order to be eligible to later receive a bonus if the referred person is ultimately hired.

All bonuses represent gross amounts. Bonus payments are taxable income. All applicable taxes will be withheld.

All new hourly, nonexempt, and exempt positions posted are eligible for bonuses in accordance with the following chart:

ONLY EXAMPLES OF THE AMOUNT
AMOUNTS MUST BE APPROVED BY THE APPROPRIATE PERSONNEL

Grade 2	$200	Grade 8–10	$1,500
Grade 3	$300	Grade 11–13	$2,000
Grade 4	$500	Grade 14	$3,000
Grade 5–7	$1,000	Grade 15 and above	$5,000

Requirements. Open positions will be posted internally.

Employees should complete the Bonus Referral Form, attach the résumé of the referred, and forward it to the HR department prior to interviewing of the prospective employee.

Referral bonuses will be paid after the new employee has worked at **(Company Name)** for 60 calendar days. Allow 30 calendar days for bonus payout.

If two or more employees refer the same candidate, the bonus will be paid to the earliest referral.

Procedures
Employee Responsibility
Complete the Bonus Referral Form. Attach résumé and/or application if available and submit to HR.

Human Resources Responsibility

Ensure that the newly referred and hired employee is employed for 60 calendar days.

Upon completion of the 60-calendar-day period, complete a check request form for the bonus amount to be payable to the referring employee.

Submit the completed check request form to the payroll department.

Payroll Responsibility

Upon receipt of the check request form, pay bonus to employee as soon as administratively feasible.

SAMPLE HIRING PROCESS AND FLOWCHART

Requirements

The Hiring Manager must have an approved Job Description (Success Profile) and requisition completed and turned into Human Resources before the recruitment process can begin. If the position is an addition to the fiscal year's approved budgeted headcount, the hiring manager must note the justification for the additional employee on the Employee Requisition Form.

Procedures

Manager Responsibility. Once a need for a position has been identified and the requisition approval has been received, the Hiring Manager and the HR representative develop a recruiting strategy.

The manager consults with the HR representative to determine appropriate sourcing methods for qualified candidates, which may include:

- Internal candidates (all jobs must be posted internally)
- Applicant Tracking System posting tools (Internet/intranet/employment boards—Monster.com, Hotjobs.com, techies.com, other such .com sites)
- College interns/college recruiting
- Employee referrals
- Industry organizations, e.g., Society of Women Engineers
- Print advertising

FIGURE 2-1. HIRING PROCESS FLOWCHART

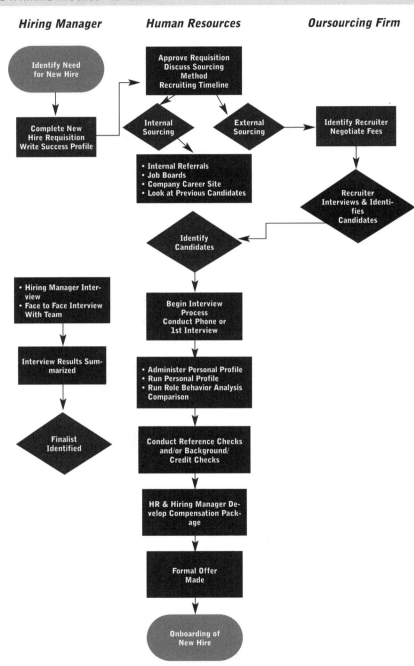

The manager reviews résumés received from the HR representative and makes the final decision on whom to formally interview. The Hiring Manager may phone-screen candidates prior to face-to-face interviews, or may request HR assistance.

The Hiring Manager also:

- Selects the interviewing team.
- Conducts formal interviews with the interviewing team.
- Collects feedback from the interviewing team and makes the hiring decision with input from the HR representative.
- Determines appropriate salary offer with input from HR representative.
- Note: All job offers require prior HR approval.
- If applicable, Hiring Manager notifies HR for basic skills testing. Basic skills testing must be completed prior to a verbal offer being made.
- Submits Payroll/Employee Change Form (ECF) to HR representative with hiring information.
- Once the candidate accepts the offer, Hiring Manager contacts internal candidates who were not hired.
- Hiring Manager should turn in all nonhired applications to HR at this time so that rejection letters may be sent out to external candidates.

Human Resources Responsibility

- Inputs the approved requisition into the Applicant Tracking System.
- Posts the job opening internally.
- Helps Hiring Manager to determine the most appropriate recruitment strategy.
- Posts on Internet/intranet and employment boards (Internet/intranet/ employment boards: Monster.com, Hotjobs.com, techies.com, or other applicable .com sites).
- If print advertising is selected, site HR representative will send job description to ad agency or newspaper for ad creation and placement.
- Evaluates and screens candidates' résumés and applications and forwards those of qualified candidates to the Hiring Manager.

> Sets up interview itineraries for candidates at request of Hiring Manager.
> Makes travel arrangements for candidate if required.
> Interviews the candidate with the rest of the interview team that the Hiring Manager chose.
> Helps Hiring Manager to make final candidate selection, if appropriate.
> Extends verbal offer to candidate. If the offer is accepted, determine start date. Typically, start dates are set for Mondays.
> Upon acceptance of job offer, contacts external candidates who were not hired via rejection letters.
> Sends out job offers (copying manager), drug testing information, new employee orientation materials, and relocation materials (if appropriate).
  > If moving a temporary employee to regular status, prepares conversion letter and provides it to manager for presentation to employee.
  > Closes job requisition in the Applicant Tracking System.
  > Removes posting on Internet/intranet and employment boards.
  > Sends out Supervisor's New-Hire Checklist.
  > Coordinates new hire orientation
> Enters new employee information into the necessary databases (e.g., payroll).
> Notifies applicable departments (IT, Facilities, and so on) of new hire.

EQUAL EMPLOYMENT OPPORTUNITY COMMISSION (EEOC) EEO-1 SURVEY

The EEO-1 Survey is an attachment to each application for employment that should be completed by any formal applicant. The information on this report is then compiled into the company's formal EEO-1 report, which must be filed with the Equal Employment Opportunity Commission each year.

What Is the EEO-1 Report?

The EEO-1 report, formally the Employer Information Report, is a government form that requires many employers to provide a count of their employees by job category and by ethnicity, race, and gender. The EEO-1 report is submitted to both the EEOC and the Department of Labor, Office of Federal Contract Compliance Programs.

Who Is Required to File the EEO-1 Report?

1. All employers with 100 or more employees
2. All federal government contractors and first-tier subcontractors with 50 or more employees *and* a contract amounting to $50,000 or more

When Must the EEO-1 Report Be Filed?

The EEO-1 report must be filed annually with the EEOC by September 30. It must use employment numbers from any pay period in July through September of that year.

The EEO-1 survey (Standard Form 100) is a survey that must be completed by companies that meet the requirements listed in the next section. This survey is required by law and is not voluntary.

Who Files the Standard Form 100

A. All private employers who are:

1. Subject to Title VII of the Civil Rights Act of 1964 (as amended by the Equal Employment Opportunity Act of 1972) with 100 or more employees EXCLUDING State and local governments, primary and secondary school systems, institutions of higher education, Indian tribes and tax-exempt private membership clubs other than labor organizations

OR

2. Subject to Title VII who have fewer than 100 employees if the company is owned or affiliated with another company, or there is centralized ownership, control or management (such as central control of personnel policies and labor relations) so that the group legally constitutes a single enterprise, and the entire enterprise employs a total of 100 or more employees

B. All federal contractors (private employers), who:

1. Are not exempt as provided for by 41 CFR 60-1.5
2. Have/has 50 or more employees, and
    a. Are prime contractors or first-tier subcontractors, and have a contract, subcontract, or purchase order of $50,000 or more
    b. Serve as a depository of government funds in any amount
    c. Is a financial institution which is an issuing and paying agent for U.S. Savings Bonds and Notes

Only those establishments located in the District of Columbia and the 50 states are required to submit Standard Form 100. No reports should be filed for establishments in Puerto Rico, the Virgin Islands, or other American Protectorates.

More information about the EEO-1 survey, including:

> How to file
> When to file
> Where to file
> Sample survey
> Race/ethnic identification
> Description of job categories

and the EEO-1 survey form may be found on the EEOC web site at http://www.eeoc.gov/employers/eeo1/index.cfm.pdf.

Instructions for the EEO-1 survey form may be found on the EEOC web site at www.eeoc.gov/stats/jobpat/e1instruct.html.

EEOC APPLICANT DATA RECORD

The EEOC Applicant Data Record is a form that is to be given with the candidate's application. The EEOC Applicant Data Record will be separated from the application and filed with all other EEOC Applicant Data Record forms. The data records are used only if the firm is audited by the EEOC.

Equal Employment Opportunity Commission (EEOC)
Applicant Data Record

Your response is voluntary and will be kept confidential, except to the extent that release may be required under applicable government regulations. You will not be subject to any adverse action if you choose not to furnish this information.

This Equal Employment Opportunity Commission information form will be kept in a confidential file separate from the accompanying application for employment.

Last Name	First Name	Initial	Date

Street Address	City	State	Zip Code

Telephone	Social Security Number

Please indicate job preference (x):

☐ Office Manger (01)
☐ Professional (02)
☐ Technician/Drafter (03)
☐ Sales (04)
☐ Office/Clerical (05)

☐ Skilled Craft Worker (06)
☐ Machine Operator (06)
☐ Assembly (07)
☐ Factory (08)
☐ Other _____

Referral Source:

☐ Advertisement
☐ Job Service

☐ Self/ Friend/ Relative Referred
☐ Other Source_____

Race/ Ethnic Group:

☐ Black
☐ Hispanic
☐ White

☐ American Indian or Alaskan Native
☐ Asia or Pacific Islander
☐ Other

Sex:

☐ Female

☐ Male

CHAPTER 3

The Interview Process

PREPARING FOR THE INTERVIEW

One of the most common mistakes that inexperienced or untrained interviewers make is to go into an interview unprepared. Most people think they are great judges of people, but after hiring a few, they tend to learn otherwise.

Never go into an interview "on the fly" just because a candidate happens to walk in the door and fill out an application. Even if you are incredibly experienced, you are still relying on your sole judgment, and your focus is less than adequate. This is not the time to wing it, or to play psychic.

Also, you should *never* rely on only one person's judgment to make a hire, no matter who that person is. Employers of choice will have a minimum of three people interview a candidate, and will have decided in advance what each one of them is going to ask. It's not a conversation. It's an interview.

So, here is how to best prepare for your next job interview.

1. Schedule an exact interview date and time, so you have time to prepare.
2. Review the job description (success profile), and identify exactly what skills, characteristics, and other job-related criteria are required.
3. Review the résumé for gaps, career changes, clarifications, and other job-related inquiries.
4. Use the candidate interview worksheet (discussed next) to prepare *specific* interview questions to ask. (A template is on the CD.)

5. Create an interview schedule, identifying who is going to interview the candidate, when they are going to do so, and which of the questions from the candidate interview worksheet each is responsible for.

6. Prepare a candidate interview folder that will include the following:

   ➤ Two copies of the job description/success profile (one each for you and the candidate)

   ➤ Application for employment (the candidate should have completed this before the interview was scheduled)

   ➤ Key contact business card of person candidate should contact

   ➤ Candidate interview worksheet (see the next section and the CD)

   ➤ Note pad (for rough, preliminary notes before completing the candidate interview worksheet)

   ➤ "Why Work Here?" takeaway (preferably in the context of a recruitment brochure)

   ➤ Organization literature

   ➤ Personal Profile and/or other behavioral assessment tool(s) (covered later in the kit)

CANDIDATE INTERVIEW WORKSHEET

This section presents a candidate interview worksheet giving sample questions for each section. You can either use these or create your own.

The form can also be found on the enclosed CD.

Candidate Interview Worksheet

Position: Customer Service Representative

Candidate: John Smith

Interviewed By: Tom Brown, Customer Relations Manager   **Date:**

Self-Assessment, Goals, and Aspirations

Q: How would you describe a successful career?

A:

Q: What is important to you in a position/job?
A:

Q: What are your long-term career goals? What are you doing to achieve those goals?
A:

Work History, Skills, Education, and Training

Q: What can you tell me about your last/present position?
A:

Q: What do you think were/are the most critical elements in successful performance at your last/current job?
A:

Q: What was your biggest accomplishment/failure in this position?
A:

Q: What training have you had to prepare you for this position?
A:

Q: Tell me about your relationship with your manager. How did/do you support him or her?
A:

Q: What do you believe qualifies you for this position?
A:

Teamwork, Manageability, and Flexibility

Q: How did you support your coworkers in your last job?
A:

Q: Describe a team experience that you found rewarding and explain why.

A:

Q: Have you ever worked in an environment that seemed to have one crisis after another? If so, how did you handle it?

A:

Q: With what type of management style do you work best?

A:

Q: Give me an example of a time when you confronted a policy with which you did not agree. What was the outcome?

A:

Analytical Problem Solving and Creativity

Q: Describe a time when you anticipated potential problems and developed preventive measures.

A:

Q: Give a specific example of a time when you used good judgment and logic in solving a problem.

A:

Q: Describe a time when you took on a project or assumed new responsibilities before you were asked to do so.

A:

Communication

Q: Tell me about a recent situation in which you had to deal with a very upset customer or coworker. What did you do to take care of this matter?

A:

Q: What is the toughest communication problem you have faced?

A:

Motivation

Q: Give an example of a time when you showed initiative and took the lead.

A:

Q: What do you need from your job in order to stay motivated?

A:

Q: Tell me about an important goal that you set in the past. Were you successful? Why?

A:

Personal/Résumé

Q: These questions must be tailored to the individual's résumé, i.e., career history, gaps in employment, and so on.

A:

Q:

A:

BEHAVIORAL INTERVIEWING GUIDE

A behavioral interview is an interview that is focused on discovering how an applicant acted in specific employment-related situations. The logic is that the candidate's past performance in previous employment roles will predict the candidate's future performance.

Instead of asking how someone might behave, you should ask how he actually did behave. You, as the interviewer, are primarily interested in how the person actually handled a situation, not in what she might hypothetically do in a particular situation.

This is a quasi-scientific methodology that is exceptionally focused on discovery, as opposed to hypothetical questions or suppositions. Interviewers who are adept at using this technique typically do not get distracted by nuances in an individual's background or gravitate to areas of commonality typically found in a candidate's résumé.

Instead, especially when it comes to legal issues that arise out of the interviewing process, the employer stays keenly focused on the skills, responsibilities, and background that are essential if a candidate is to be successful in this specific role within your specific company. This is the most legally defensible interviewing process used by employers today.

What follows are the success profile for a controller position and behavioral interviewing guides for the technical skills (or hard skills) that an individual must have to perform this particular role and for the "performance skills" (or softer human skills) that are essential to success within this position. The examples given here would be used by an employer to select one of the candidates for this position.

Be aware that a behavioral interviewing guide should be developed for every role in your organization. This can be slowly integrated into your best practices if you develop these tools for each position as that position becomes available. This is one of the most powerful and revealing interviewing processes used because it focuses on the behavior and not the candidate. It is used extensively by employers who are noted for having exceptionally high-performing workforces.

Success Profile—Controller/Manager

Position Title: Controller/Manager	Reports to: CFO
Department or Job Family: Finance	Approved by:
Date Modified:	Modified by:
Compensation Strategy:	FSLA Status:

ABOUT YOUR COMPANY:

_____ was founded in 19__ by IT professionals who recognized a need for high-quality IT infrastructure and operations management technologies, best practices in process and implementation, and specialists who are experts in their design, implementation, and use. Recently listed as one of the *Inc.* 500 fastest-growing privately held companies, _____ helps IT organizations extend their service capabilities, and was recently named _____ 's Business Technology Optimization Software partner of the year.

PURPOSE/MISSION:

Provide leadership and coordination of Finance Department operations, financial statement closing, and budget management functions. Ensure that company accounting procedures conform to generally accepted accounting principles.

PRIMARY RESPONSIBILITIES:

➤ Oversee and participate in the monthly financial statement closing process and produce accurate financial statements on a timely basis.

➤ Implement appropriate accounting policies and procedures to ensure that adequate internal controls over accounting processes exist and that all transactions are reported in accordance with GAAP.

➤ Oversee cash management, including the preparation of weekly cash status reports and rolling cash flow projections.

➤ Review and analyze monthly operating results against budget.

➤ Oversee the daily operations of the finance department.

➤ Assist in the preparation of financial forecasts.

➤ Ensure compliance with local, state, and federal regulatory requirements.

➤ Establish and implement short- and long-range departmental goals, objectives, policies, and operating procedures.

➤ Direct financial audits and provide recommendations for procedural improvements.

➤ Other duties as assigned.

PERFORMANCE SKILLS:

➤ Attention to detail

➤ Commitment to task

➤ Initiative

➤ Integrity

➤ Teamwork

➤ Policies, processes, and procedures

➤ Quality

➤ Systematic problem solving

➤ Planning, prioritizing, and goal setting

➤ Communication

➤ Continuous learning

EDUCATION/EXPERIENCE REQUIREMENTS:

➤ Bachelor's degree in accounting and at least six years' experience in accounting with demonstrated progressive responsibility; CPA preferred. Previous staff management experience is required.

➤ Knowledge of finance, accounting, budgeting, and cost control principles, including generally accepted accounting principles. Knowledge of automated financial and accounting reporting systems. Knowledge of federal and state financial regulations.

➤ Ability to analyze financial data and prepare financial reports, statements, and projections. Working knowledge of short- and long-term budgeting and forecasting, rolling budgets, and product-line profitability analysis.

➤ Excellent professional written and verbal communication and interpersonal skills. Ability to motivate teams to produce high-quality materials within tight time frames and manage several projects simultaneously. Ability to participate in and facilitate group meetings.

➤ Proficiency with personal computing applications as well as specific financial accounting applications.

➤ Desire and ability to be both hands-on and an effective delegator and manager.

Technical Skills Questions (Sample)

Technical Skills Interview Guide

Position: *Controller*   **Candidate Name:** _____

Date: ___ / ___ / ___   **Interviewer Name:** _____

Check marks indicate the skills that you will interview for	Very Strong Evidence Skill Is Not Present	Strong Evidence Skill Is Not Present	Some Evidence Skill Is Present	Strong Evidence Skill Is Present	Very Strong Evidence Skill Is Present	Insufficient Evidence For or Against Skill
☑ Corporate governance						
☑ Business Integration Strategy						
☑ Finance, accounting, and tax						
☑ Budgeting, forecasting, and reporting						
☑ Processes and systems						
☑ Legal						
☑ HR						
☑ MIS						
☑ Purchasing						

Corporate Governance
➤ Establish corporate governance program.
➤ Establish internal control system.

EXAMPLE QUESTION

☐ Describe a time when you had to set the corporate governance objectives, tone, policies, risk appetite, and accountabilities for the organization and then monitor the performance against those objectives. How did you create a companywide focus on corporate governance, risk management, and ethics compliance through a Governance Risk Compliance Operating Model?

For a comprehensive list of behavioral questions, see the enclosed CD.

Business Integration Strategy
➤ Implement a value chain analysis or balanced scorecard system.
➤ Assess strategic investments.
➤ Evaluate core businesses and product lines.
➤ Develop relationships with third parties that accelerate key business strategies.

EXAMPLE QUESTION

☐ Describe a time when you had to identify appropriate vendors to help the company implement a balanced scorecard or other similar program that provides a bridge between operational data, business drivers, strategic planning, and the demands of customers.

For a comprehensive list of behavioral questions, see the enclosed CD.

Finance, Accounting, and Tax
➤ Develop a finance strategy.
➤ Create a cash management program.
➤ Research and implement solutions to complex accounting and tax issues.
➤ Create spreadsheets for stock-based compensation.

EXAMPLE QUESTION

☐ Tell me about a time when you were asked to develop a financing strategy for the enterprise.

For a comprehensive list of behavioral questions, see the enclosed CD.

Budgeting, Forecasting, and Reporting

➤ Identify potential new investors.

➤ Create powerful and concise PowerPoint presentations.

➤ Communicate financial information to the CEO and the board.

➤ Assess enterprise risk.

EXAMPLE QUESTION

❑ Share with me how you have developed detailed budgets and forecasts that can be quickly manipulated to change data and key elements to produce multiple scenarios for decision-making purposes.

For a comprehensive list of behavioral questions, see the enclosed CD.

Processes and Systems

➤ Optimize organization of the finance/accounting department.

➤ Coordinate efforts with MIS, HR, accounting, engineering, and sales systems.

➤ Create, process, and review all accounting entries made to the general ledger system.

➤ Communicate information across the enterprise.

EXAMPLE QUESTION

❑ Describe to me how you organized your accounting department and what recommendations you made for changing legacy systems.

For a comprehensive list of behavioral questions, see the enclosed CD.

Legal

➤ Have the ability to negotiate agreements, including software license agreements, service agreements, and confidentiality and nondisclosure agreements.

➤ Have the ability to assess both legal and business risks, identify potential mitigating actions, and effectively communicate solutions requiring approval.

➤ Have the ability to understand the practical implications of contracts for the financial health of the organization (e.g., revenue recognition issues and long-term objectives).

EXAMPLE QUESTION

❑ Describe your experience in the management or negotiation of contracts or agreements, specifically software license agreements, service agreements, and confidentiality or nondisclosure agreements.

For a comprehensive list of behavioral questions, see the enclosed CD.

HR

➤ Have the ability to manage and facilitate employee recruitment and selection.
➤ Have the ability to manage rewards strategy, including employee compensation and benefits.
➤ Have the ability to communicate HR issues and solutions effectively to the entire enterprise.
➤ Have the ability to create and implement HR policies for the entire organization.

EXAMPLE QUESTION

☐ Describe your experience in the management of human resources. Describe your experience with recruitment, compensation, and benefits.

For a comprehensive list of behavioral questions, see the enclosed CD.

MIS

➤ Have the ability to manage and facilitate MIS support services.
➤ Have the ability to manage MIS systems.

EXAMPLE QUESTION

☐ Describe your experience in the management of the MIS function. Describe your experience with software selection and implementation, and with hardware selection and implementation. Were there any unique features or requirements for your software and/or hardware systems or packages? What were they?

For a comprehensive list of behavioral questions, see the enclosed CD.

Purchasing

➤ Ability to manage the purchasing process, including oversight of the purchase order approval process and review and reduction of direct and indirect purchases.

EXAMPLE QUESTIONS

☐ Describe your experience in the management of the purchasing function.

For a comprehensive list of behavioral questions, see the enclosed CD.

The Behavioral Interviewing Guide—Performance Skill Questions (Sample)

Performance Skills Interview Guide

Position: *Controller*   **Candidate Name:** _____
Date: ___ / ___ / ___   **Interviewer Name:** _____

Check marks indicate the skills that you will interview for	Very Strong Evidence Skill Is Not Present	Strong Evidence Skill Is Not Present	Some Evidence Skill Is Present	Strong Evidence Skill Is Present	Very Strong Evidence Skill Is Present	Insufficient Evidence For or Against Skill
☑ Attention to detail						
☑ Integrity						
☑ Policies, processes, and procedures						
☑ Commitment to task						
☑ Quality						
☑ Initiative						
☑ Negotiating						
☑ Communication						
☑ Systematic problem solving						
☑ Teamwork						
☑ Energizing others						
☑ Decision making and problem solving						
☑ Planning, prioritizing, and goal setting						

Summary and Recommendation:
☐ Schedule another interview
☐ Check references
☐ Hire
☐ Do not hire

Comments:

Very Strong Evidence Skill Is Not Present	Strong Evidence Skill Is Not Present	Some Evidence Skill Is Present	Strong Evidence Skill Is Present	Very Strong Evidence Skill Is Present	Insufficient Evidence For or Against Skill

Attention to Detail
➤ Able to be alert in a high-risk environment.
➤ Able to follow detailed procedures and ensure accuracy in documentation and data.
➤ Able to carefully monitor gauges, instruments, or processes; concentrate on routine work details.
➤ Able to organize and maintain a system of records.

EXAMPLE QUESTION

☐ Describe something you've done that underscores your commitment to being attentive to detail in an environment where confidentiality is required and a high degree of time pressure is exerted upon you to get a work product out to important clients.

For a comprehensive list of behavioral questions, see the enclosed CD.

Integrity
➤ Accepts responsibility for own actions and events, even when mistakes have been made.
➤ Avoids taking credit for others' work and shares credit with others when deserved.
➤ Demonstrates concern for how personal values and beliefs are shown through on-the-job behavior.
➤ Does not compromise principles, even if detrimental to own goals.
➤ Practices what he or she preaches, with actions matching words.
➤ Maintains confidences.
➤ Handles all situations honestly and promotes an ethical work environment.

EXAMPLE QUESTION

☐ Describe a time when you chose to be honest, even though being quiet or agreeable might have been easier, particularly in a period of intense competition or rapid change.

For a comprehensive list of behavioral questions, see the enclosed CD.

Policies, Processes, and Procedures
➤ Able to act in accordance with established guidelines and follow standard procedures in crisis situations.
➤ Able to communicate and enforce organizational policies and procedures.
➤ Able to recognize and constructively conform to unwritten rules or practices.

EXAMPLE QUESTION

☐ On some jobs, it is necessary to act strictly in accordance with policy. Give me an example of a situation when you were expected to act in accordance with policy even when it was not convenient. What did you do?

For a comprehensive list of behavioral questions, see the enclosed CD.

Commitment to Task

➤ Able to take responsibility for actions and outcomes and persist despite obstacles.
➤ Available around the clock in case of emergency.
➤ Able to give long hours to the job.
➤ Demonstrates dependability in difficult circumstances and shows a sense of urgency about getting results.

EXAMPLE QUESTION

☐ Describe a difficult situation in which you took full responsibility for the actions and outcomes of your team and your coordinated work product. How did you act on this?

For a comprehensive list of behavioral questions, see the enclosed CD.

Quality

➤ Able to maintain high standards despite pressing deadlines.
➤ Establishes high standards and measures.
➤ Does work right the first time and inspects material for flaws.
➤ Tests new methods thoroughly.
➤ Reinforces excellence as a fundamental priority.

EXAMPLE QUESTION

☐ Describe a situation in which a crucial deadline was nearing, but you didn't want to compromise quality. How did you deal with it? How did you motivate others to contribute?

For a comprehensive list of behavioral questions, see the enclosed CD.

Initiative

➤ Able to bring about great results in ordinary circumstances.
➤ Able to prepare for problems or opportunities in advance.
➤ Able to transform leads into productive business outcomes.
➤ Able to undertake additional responsibilities and respond to situations as they arise without supervision.

EXAMPLE QUESTION

☐ Tell me about a situation in which you aggressively capitalized on an opportunity to have a positive impact on the financial stability of a company and converted something ordinary into something special.

For a comprehensive list of behavioral questions, see the enclosed CD.

Negotiating

- Able to obtain agreement among multiple parties.
- Earns trust while working out a deal.
- Uses good timing and carefully calculated strategies when bargaining.
- Communicates high value of services based on understanding of the party's wants, needs, and problems.
- Identifies and addresses hidden agendas.
- Makes a clear connection between value, benefits, and cost.

EXAMPLE QUESTION

> ☐ Think of a time when you identified the hidden agenda of someone with whom you were negotiating (i.e., for a credit facility, lease, or something else). How did you work with that agenda to achieve a successful outcome for the business?

For a comprehensive list of behavioral questions, see the enclosed CD.

Communication

- Conveys information clearly, concisely, and logically, both in writing and verbally.
- Adjusts the delivery of communication so that the listener is engaged and understands the message.
- Listens actively, avoids interrupting, and gives full attention to the speaker.
- Correctly interprets complex information and asks questions to check own understanding.
- Selects the best medium (verbal, written, e-mail, voicemail, or other) for the message to be communicated.
- Recognizes the nonverbal reactions of others; looks for clues to how others think or feel; demonstrates sensitivity toward and understanding of others' feelings.

EXAMPLE QUESTION

> ☐ Describe a challenging time when others relied on you to interpret information or provide clarification in the absence of the CEO or other key management team members.

For a comprehensive list of behavioral questions, see the enclosed CD.

Systematic Problem Solving

- Able to apply systems thinking to generate solutions.
- Able to focus on process rather than isolated events.
- Able to obtain multiple assessments of a situation and be systematic in identifying trouble spots.
- Able to use tools to define problems and evaluate alternative solutions.

EXAMPLE QUESTION

> ☐ Solving a problem often necessitates evaluation of alternative solutions. Give me an example of a time when you actively defined several solutions to a single problem. Did you use any tools such as research, brainstorming, or mathematics?

For a comprehensive list of behavioral questions, see the enclosed CD.

Teamwork
➤ Defines the team beyond the immediate circle of coworkers, working closely with other departments.
➤ Shares credit appropriately with others.
➤ Notices when others need help and offers assistance without being asked.
➤ Shares information appropriately with others on the job.
➤ Expresses appreciation for and acknowledges the value of team members' perspectives and contribution.
➤ Involves team members to obtain differing perspectives, ideas, opinions, expertise, and support.
➤ Works effectively and cooperatively with others and promotes a cooperative and positive working environment.
➤ Places higher priority on team or organizational goals than on own goals.

EXAMPLE QUESTION

> ☐ Describe a time when you were praised individually for something to which a whole team contributed. What did you do to ensure that the rest of the team members received due credit?

For a comprehensive list of behavioral questions, see the enclosed CD.

Energizing Others
➤ Able to exhibit a "can-do" approach and inspire associates to excel.
➤ Able to use competition to encourage others.
➤ Able to develop performance standards and confront negative attitudes.
➤ Able to develop team spirit.

EXAMPLE QUESTION

> ☐ Describe a situation in which your work group succeeded because you exhibited a positive, "can-do" approach in guiding them.

For a comprehensive list of behavioral questions, see the enclosed CD.

Decision Making and Problem Solving

➤ Able to take action in solving problems while exhibiting judgment and a realistic understanding of issues.

➤ Able to use reason, even when dealing with emotional topics.

➤ Able to review facts and weigh options.

EXAMPLE QUESTION

> ☐ Having a good solution for a problem often entails more than just being intelligent. Often, exercise of good judgment is needed to complement logic in choosing a practical solution. Describe a situation in which you used good judgment in solving a problem.

For a comprehensive list of behavioral questions, see the enclosed CD.

Planning, Prioritizing, and Goal Setting

➤ Establishes a systematic course of action so that work is completed in a timely way while maintaining quality and cost requirements.

➤ Identifies the most and least important assignments and adjusts priorities when needed.

➤ Anticipates obstacles and plans for contingencies in getting work completed.

➤ Coordinates plans with internal and external partners, avoiding scheduling conflicts.

➤ Allocates sufficient time for completing work.

➤ Creates and uses written plans with specific goals, timelines, and target dates.

➤ Keeps noncritical issues and distractions from interfering with work completion.

EXAMPLE QUESTION

> ☐ Describe a time when you forecasted several years out to identify what sales, revenues, associated costs, and related gross margins would be. How did you put your organization in a position to access the greatest revenues with the highest gross margins?

For a comprehensive list of behavioral questions, see the enclosed CD.

CHAPTER 4

Conducting the Interview

BEST PRACTICES IN CONDUCTING THE INTERVIEW

Ensure that the Environment Is Conducive to an Effective Interview

It should be quiet, with no distractions, private, and comfortable.

Turn off your cell phone, reroute all calls, and do not allow interruptions unless it's an absolute emergency. Remember, recruitment is PR and sales. Would you interrupt a customer? If the candidate feels unimportant or disrespected during the interview, imagine how he assumes he will be treated if he is hired.

Manage the Candidate's Expectations

Welcome her, put her at ease, and then give her the lay of the land. For example:

Welcome to _____. I hope you found us OK [or some other small talk]. To put you at ease, let me tell you exactly what to expect, and how the interview process will roll out.

As you can see from the interview schedule, you will be seeing _____ and _____, and we want you to get to know us as well as we want to get to know you.

I will start by asking you some questions about your background and experience, and then I will answer any questions you may have about our organization, the job, and so on. (*Note: This is a critical statement because you do* not *want the candidate interviewing you before you interview him. This sets the scene to prevent that from happening. If it happens anyway, just say, "I'll be happy to answer all of your questions before we are done, but for now, . . .")*

Also, tell the candidate that you will be taking notes so that she is not distracted or put off by it when you do. (More on note taking later.)

Ask the First Question

The first question you should *always* ask *every* candidate is: "Tell me about yourself!"

Because this question is so open-ended, not only is it a good test of the candidate's thinking, judgment, and communication skills, but it is usually a great source of material for follow-up questions, as well. Unless the response is of great value, try to get the candidate to limit it to less than five minutes. Some inexperienced or nervous candidates will ramble on forever into totally irrelevant territory (again a reflection of their judgment and emotional intelligence). By the same token, you may uncover some really juicy information that you never even asked for.

There is actually a format that can be followed for the response to this question, called the 4Es. That is:

*E*arly life

*E*ducation

*E*xperience

*E*xpectations

Can you see how this creates a nice, neat little chronology of who this person is? The challenge is to keep the response crisp and relevant, ideally less than three minutes long.

80/20 Rule

You should be talking no more than 20 percent of the time, and the candidate should be talking no less than 80 percent of the time. The more you talk, the less you learn about the candidate. This is why God created us with two ears and only one mouth.

This is another very common mistake of inexperienced interviewers. Between wanting to tell the candidate all about the organization, yourself, and the job, and being nervous yourself, the tendency is to talk too much.

Another contributor to this phenomenon is the discomfort of silence, which leads us to the next principle.

Use Open-Ended Questions, Clarifying Questions, and Silence

Open-Ended Questions. In addition to the "tell me about yourself" question, you should ask similar open-ended questions throughout the interview. Open-ended questions cannot be answered with a simple yes or no.

For example, rather than asking if the candidate has ever dealt with a dissatisfied customer, which could be answered with a simple yes or no, ask: "Can you tell me about a time when you had to deal with a dissatisfied customer, and how you handled it?"

Clarifying Questions. Some of the most powerful and revealing information does not come from the candidate's first response to a question. It comes from a clarifying question. For example, using the previous question, once the candidate gives you his initial response, do not go right to the next question. Rather, use a clarifying question such as:

- ➤ Tell me more!
- ➤ And?
- ➤ Why's that?
- ➤ It sounds like there's a lot more to that story.
- ➤ In what way?
- ➤ How so?
- ➤ Is there anything else I should know?

Can you see how these comebacks can elicit some real meat? These clarifying questions require the candidate to dig deeper, to improvise, and to go beyond his standard shtick. There are tons more of them, but you get the idea.

Silence Is Golden. You have probably figured this one out by now. As we mentioned earlier, do not fall victim to the novice's need to fill in silence with more questions or statements. This is another extension of the 80/20 rule.

It is OK to wait a few seconds after the candidate "thinks" that she has answered the question. Just like the clarifying questions, waiting a few seconds can also elicit more information because, just like you, the candidate is nervous, and will want to fill in that awkward silence with something. And that's the real test.

Take Notes

As mentioned earlier, let the candidate know during the setup that you will be taking notes, so that you do not forget important information. However, there is also an art to note taking.

If the candidate tells you something particularly noteworthy (good *or* bad), like, "I punched the boss at my last job," *do not* immediately start scribbling "he punched the boss" in your notes. By doing so, you are giving the candidate immediate feedback that he has just said something noteworthy. If it was something good, then you will get a whole bunch more. If it was something bad, then you have tipped him off to put a lid on it.

Rather, wait 30 seconds, and then casually jot down a few words to remind yourself later what the candidate said. It is not important that your notes be full sentences. It is not important that you write cleanly between the lines. That's why you have a note pad in your candidate interview folder.

What *is* important is that you capture the thought and do not create a distraction or a tip-off in the process. Timing is everything. When the interview is over, you can edit and paraphrase your notes onto the candidate interview worksheet and candidate assessment form. (Both of these can be found on the CD.)

LEGALITIES OF INTERVIEWING

Never Ask Illegal Questions, and Avoid Inappropriate Ones

Inexperienced interviewers are always nervous about what they can or cannot ask a candidate. Most people know the obvious illegal areas, such as race, sex, religion, national origin, and sexual preference, but few are aware of the more borderline or gray-area questions that may also be construed as being either illegal or at least inappropriate.

For example, asking a candidate where she lives, what nationality her name is, or about her family history is off-limits. It may seem chummy to you, but for some, it is an invasion. There was a time when employers would ask a candidate if he was married, had kids, was buying his home, and other such questions, under the erroneous and outdated assumption that these things automatically translated into stability.

We know better now. You might find a single, childless person who rents an apartment who is less stressed out than the stereotypical family person with all the burdens and responsibilities that come with spouses, houses, and kids. The bottom line: It's irrelevant, and it's illegal.

Rule of thumb: Whenever you are unsure, always ask yourself: "Is this question job-related?"

In other words, is it a predictor of success on the job? Then, "When in doubt, leave it out!"

This doesn't have to be rocket science. If you just ask yourself, "Is this question job-related?" it will keep you out of hot water 99 percent of the time. There are plenty of other relevant and informative questions that you can and should ask that you will discover later in this kit.

What Not to Ask

There are many questions that you should not ask during a job interview, even if your motives are innocent. This is because they can make you vulnerable to charges of discrimination if the prospective employee is not hired. You also have to be careful about information that is volunteered by potential employees for the same reason. Most illegal interview questions are unrelated to any legitimate hiring criteria, so just stay focused on relevant issues such as education, work-related skills, and work history.

Never use the word *disabled* or *handicapped* in a job interview. However, physical capabilities may be directly relevant to job performance in certain types of jobs. In such a case, ask whether the candidate is capable of performing the particular job duties.

You should also steer clear of questions about an applicant's medical history or whether the applicant has previously received workers' compensation. These questions are regarded as potential surrogates for inquiries about disability status.

Here are some general questions that should *never* be asked at any point during the interview process. Keep the focus of the interview questions on the skill and experience level of the candidate and the qualifications needed to perform the job.

- How old are you?
- Do you have any disabilities?
- Are you handicapped?
- Are you pregnant?
- Do you plan on having children?
- Are you married with children?
- Have you ever been arrested?
- What is your religious affiliation?
- What is your sexual orientation?
- What is your ethnic background?

The Not-so-Obvious Illegal Questions That Can Cause Major Problems

Unfortunately, most hiring managers are untrained in the legalities of interviewing, so it's fairly common for candidates to be asked illegal questions.

Virtually all states have laws or regulations prohibiting discrimination on the basis of race, color, religion, national origin, ancestry, medical condition, physical handicap, marital status, and age (40+).

Generally, questions on employment applications or in interviews about national origin (including questions about the applicant's native language) are illegal. Employers also can't ask about marital status or the number and ages of children and dependents. Nor can you ask questions about pregnancy, birth-control use, or plans for having children.

Employers *can* ask about disabilities in the following form: "Do you have any physical condition that may limit your ability to perform the job for which you're applying? If yes, what can be done to accommodate your limitations?"

You *can't*, however, ask about an applicant's general medical condition or illnesses, or whether he's received workers' compensation. Nor can you ask, "Do you have any physical disabilities or handicaps?"

Employers also aren't allowed to inquire about religion. A question such as, "Are there any holidays or days of the week that you can't work?" would probably be held to be illegal, even if religion wasn't mentioned. However, it would probably be acceptable to ask, "We often work holidays and weekends. Is there anything that would prevent you from doing so?"

Employers can ask if an applicant has ever been convicted of a felony, but not if she has ever been arrested. In some states, even questions about a felony conviction would have to be worded carefully to make sure that they're clearly job-related. For example, a candidate for controller might be asked, "Have you ever been convicted of embezzlement?" but not, "Have you ever been convicted of a felony?"

Legal Questions—What You Can Ask About and When It Is Legal to Do So

Table 4-1 gives some questions on a number of topics that you can and can't ask and some things that you can or can't do.

TABLE 4-1

Subject	*Can* Do or Ask	*Cannot* Do or Ask
Age	Ask age after hiring the applicant. Are you over 18?	How old are you? Employer cannot estimate age.
Children	After hiring, ask the number and ages of children for insurance purposes.	Do you have children at home? How old are they? Who cares for them? Do you plan on having more?
Citizenship	Whether or not applicant is a U.S. citizen or legally eligible to work in the United States under the Immigration Reform and Control Act.	Make personal inquiries into applicant's heritage.
Criminal record	If security clearance is necessary, can this be achieved?	Have you ever been arrested, convicted, or spent time in jail prior to employment?

TABLE 4-1 (CONTINUED)

Subject	*Can* Do or Ask	*Cannot* Do or Ask
Disability	Are you able to carry out the necessary job assignments and perform them well and safely?	What are the nature and/or severity of any disabilities that you have?
Driver's license	Can ask applicant about driving status and request a Department of Motor Vehicles printout only if the position requires driving.	Have you ever had a speeding ticket? (Unless the job requires a clean driving record, like an over the road (OTR) driver or other Department of Transportation–licensed professional driver.)
Education	Inquire about education and/or certificates for positions requiring them.	Readily inquire about a high school diploma for entry-level or remedial positions.
Financial status	Employer can request necessary financial information for benefits, stock options, and 401(k) after applicant is hired and at applicant's discretion.	Employer may not inquire about financial status, wage attachments, outstanding loans or obligations, or bankruptcy status.
Housing	If you have no phone, how can we reach you?	If you have no phone, how can we contact you?
Marital status	After hiring, ask status for insurance purposes.	Are you married, single, engaged, or divorced? Are you currently living with anyone? Do you see your ex-spouse?
Military status	Are you a veteran? Why not? Do you have any job-related experience in the military?	What is your discharge status? What branch did you serve in?
Physical data	Explain manual labor, lifting, and other job requirements. Employer may also demonstrate these duties and require applicant to undergo a physical examination.	How tall are you? How heavy are you?
Race	Employer may notice general distinguishing characteristics to be used for identification purposes.	Question applicant on eye color or hair color, or ask any other direct or indirect questions indicating race or status.
References	Who referred you for a position here? Ask for past employment references.	Require the submission of a religious reference.
Relatives	Once employed, employer may ask for a person to contact in case of an emergency.	Employer cannot inquire about nearest relative or next of kin.
Sex	Interviewer may notice general appearance.	Make comments or notes unless sex is a bona fide occupational qualification.
Social security	Once an applicant is hired, her employer may request the applicant's social security number for benefits purposes.	Interviewer cannot ask an elderly applicant whether she is receiving social security benefits.
Union affiliation	Employer can notify applicants of the corporation's union status.	Interviewer cannot ask whether the applicant has ever been affiliated with a union.

GUT WRENCHERS: *THE 50 TOUGHEST QUESTIONS YOU'LL EVER GET OR GIVE IN A JOB INTERVIEW*

As former outplacement counselors, we created these questions for our clients to practice in advance. Every one of these questions should be answered both positively and in job-related terms. That was Rule 1 for interviewees. Try some of these yourself, and see how your answers would resonate with you!

1. Tell me about yourself.
2. Why do you want to work here?
3. What are your strengths?
4. What are your weaknesses?
5. What do you know about us?
6. Why should I hire you?
7. Why did you (or why do you want to) leave your current employer?
8. If you could turn back time and live your life over, what would you do differently?
9. Describe the ideal work environment for you.
10. Tell me about the worst boss you ever had.
11. If you could change one thing about your last (current) job, what would it be?
12. How do you think your coworkers would describe you, both good and bad?
13. How do you think your bosses would describe you, both good and bad?
14. In prior performance reviews, what were your opportunities for improvement?
15. What are your greatest accomplishments so far?
16. Describe yourself in three words.
17. Are you interested in managing or leading others? Why or why not?
18. How do you define success?
19. Besides money, what do you value or need most if you are to have job satisfaction?
20. Have you ever been fired (laid off, outplaced, etc.)? Explain the circumstances.
21. If you gave your last boss a performance review, what would he or she need to change?

22. Do you prefer to work alone or with others? Why?
23. Describe a difficult situation or task that you had to deal with, and how you did so.
24. How do you feel about travel or relocation?
25. Is there anything that would physically or mentally prevent you from performing this job?
26. What other organizations are you pursuing, or are pursuing you?
27. Do you consider yourself to be creative? If so, give some examples.
28. How would you describe your personality?
29. How much are you expecting to earn in this job?
30. How do you feel about incentives, which are heavily tied to performance?
31. How do you feel about psychological tests?
32. How do you feel about drug tests?
33. What are your goals for five years and ten years out?
34. Do you prefer a job with clearly defined tasks, or one that is more self-directed?
35. Do you prefer to work for a man or a woman? Why?
36. How do you feel about working in a diverse workplace (with minorities, for example)?
37. If you could change three things about yourself, what would they be?
38. Do you consider yourself to be a traditionalist? Why or why not?
39. What motivates you?
40. Do you think that people are basically lazy and need to be pushed to perform?
41. Have you ever had to fire someone? Explain why and how you did it.
42. If you could be in your own business, what business would it be?
43. Do you consider yourself to be more of a people person or a taskmaster?
44. What qualities do you think are necessary to be a leader?
45. How long do you anticipate being in this job, or with our organization?
46. Do you believe that success depends more on what you know than on whom you know?
47. How do you perform under stress?
48. Do you keep current in your field? How?

49. Do you have any role models? If so, who are they, and why are they role models?
50. What more would you like to know about the job, or about this organization?

INTERVIEW QUESTIONS BY CATEGORY

Self-Assessment

➤ What are your greatest strengths? How have you used them?
➤ In what areas would you like to improve? Why?
➤ How would you describe a successful career?
➤ Tell me about a time when you missed an obvious solution to a problem.
➤ How would your references describe you?
➤ What applicable attributes or experience do you have?
➤ Why are you the best person for this job?

Work History

➤ What can you tell me about your last/present position?
➤ What were your expectations of your last/current job? To what extent were/are they met?
➤ What were your starting and ending/current levels of compensation?
➤ What were/are your responsibilities?
➤ How would you describe a typical workday?
➤ What was your biggest accomplishment/failure in this position?
➤ What was/is it like working for your manager? What were/are his or her strengths and weaknesses?
➤ Tell me about your relationship with your manager. How did/do you support him or her?
➤ How has your supervisor supported your performance?
➤ What do you think were/are the most critical elements of successfully performing your last/current job?
➤ Why are you leaving your current employer?
➤ How have your previous jobs prepared you for more responsibility?

➤ What major challenges and problems have you faced? How did you handle them?

➤ What job have you had that was most/least rewarding?

➤ How would you describe your ideal job?

Education and Training

➤ How would you describe your academic achievements?

➤ What subjects did you enjoy or excel in most? Why?

➤ How has your education and training contributed to your success?

➤ What training have you had to prepare you for this position?

Goals and Aspirations

➤ What is important to you in a position/job?

➤ What are your long-term career goals? What are you doing to achieve those goals?

➤ How will this position help you reach those goals?

➤ How does your past/current job relate to the overall goals of the organization?

➤ What are you looking for in your next job? What's important to you?

➤ What do you do to stay informed about your organization and the industry?

Skills Matching

➤ Tell me in detail about your *(skill)* experience.

➤ What exposure to/experience with *(skill)* have you had?

➤ Please give me an example of how you've used *(skill)*.

➤ What do you believe qualifies you for this position?

➤ Tell me what interests you about this position.

➤ What elements of this position would be new to you?

Analytical/Problem Solving

➤ Give me an example of a problem you faced and describe what you did to solve it.

➢ Describe a situation in which you had to make a quick decision.

➢ Tell me how you analyze data or information to solve problems.

➢ Describe a time when you anticipated potential problems and developed preventive measures.

➢ Give a specific example of a time when you used good judgment and logic in solving a problem.

Teamwork

➢ What did you do in your last job to contribute to a team-oriented environment?

➢ How did you support your coworkers in your last job?

➢ What challenges have you faced when trying to work with teams? How have you handled those challenges?

➢ Describe a team experience that you found rewarding and explain why.

Flexibility

➢ How do you overcome objections to your ideas or suggestions?

➢ How do you handle unexpected interruptions to your schedule?

➢ Have you ever worked in an environment that seemed to have one crisis after another? If so, how did you handle it?

➢ Tell me about the most difficult or frustrating individual that you've ever had to work with and how you worked with that person.

Verbal Communication

➢ What is the toughest communication problem you have faced?

➢ Describe how you gather information and input from others.

➢ Tell about a time that you positively influenced the actions of others.

➢ Tell me about a recent situation in which you had to deal with a very upset customer or coworker. What did you do to take care of this matter?

Written Communication

➢ Describe the most significant written document/report/presentation you have had to complete.

➤ In any of your positions, in what situations was written communication better? In what situations was verbal communication better?

Organization and Planning

➤ How do you plan projects to meet deadlines? How do you avoid interruptions?
➤ What organization systems do you use to plan your work or projects?
➤ Describe how you organize your workday so that you are most productive.

Manageability

➤ How do you respond to criticism?
➤ With what type of management style do you work best?
➤ What disagreements have you had with a supervisor? How did you resolve?
➤ Give me an example of a time when you confronted a policy with which you did not agree. What was the outcome?
➤ Describe the most effective way in which a supervisor could give you direction.

Creativity

➤ Tell me about a time when you went above and beyond your normal responsibilities to complete your job.
➤ Describe the most creative project or solution you have developed.
➤ How do you handle situations that require decisions or actions when there is no set procedure to follow?
➤ Describe a time when you took on a project or assumed new responsibilities before you were asked to do so.

Motivation

➤ Give an example of a time when you showed initiative and took the lead.
➤ What do you need from your job in order to stay motivated?
➤ Describe a time when you set your sights too high or too low.
➤ How would you define success for someone in this position?
➤ Tell me about an important goal that you set in the past. Were you successful? Why?

General Questions

- What interests you about this job?
- What qualifies you for this position?
- What do you know about this organization?
- Why do you want to work for us?
- What can you contribute to this organization?
- What motivates you?

Clarifying Questions

- Tell me more.
- Why's that?
- And?
- In what way?
- How so?
- Anything else?

Clerical Interview Questions

- Describe a typical workday.
- What skills can you bring to this job?
- Describe the accomplishments of which you are most proud.
- What aspects of your job do you enjoy most; which cause the most problems?
- What software programs have you used? What activities have you performed with them?
- How many people do you support?
- Describe what you do when the needs of your supervisors conflict.
- Tell me what organizational systems or processes you use to prioritize your work and your day.

Management Interview Questions

- How many people have you managed at one time? What levels of employees were they?
- Describe your current management responsibilities.

- What types of decisions are beyond your authority?
- What is the level of your budget responsibility?
- What was the most expensive fiscal mistake that you have ever made?
- What are some tasks that you typically delegate?
- Give an example of a time when you delegated effectively.
- What feedback have you received from those you have managed? Give me some examples of your strengths and areas that need development.
- How do you keep your staff aware of the organization's information and activities?
- What management situation is most difficult for you?
- How have you successfully set objectives for your team?
- How do you handle poor performance?
- How do you develop the members of your staff to improve their performance?
- How would you describe your management style?
- How many people have you hired? Describe your process for selecting a new employee.
- Tell me about your biggest hiring success/mistake.
- What was the turnover rate in your department/organization last year?
- What steps do you take before deciding to terminate an employee?

THE FIVE MOST COMMON INTERVIEWER ERRORS

1. Halo or Horns

Inexperienced interviewers (and people in general) have great difficulty withholding judgment on a candidate until after the interview is over, and therefore are subject to selective perception once they have made their prejudgment.

For example, you might see that a candidate went to the same school as you did, which may make a favorable first impression on you and then overshadow certain negatives that might disqualify other candidates. In other words, this person has a "halo" over her from that point on. This is normal and human, but wrong.

The same phenomenon occurs when someone has "horns." Perhaps he went to a rival school, or he doesn't have the same style of dress as you, or there is some other *non-job-related* criterion that overshadows your objectivity and judgment.

This is another good reason for using multiple interviewers: to check and balance each other and keep each other honest.

2. Contrast Error

They say that if you hang around with fat people, you will look skinnier. Or if you hang around with ugly people, you will appear prettier. The same holds true if you interview a bunch of losers, and then a mediocre or average candidate comes in; suddenly you are relieved that she is not a dog.

The tendency in this case is to see the lesser of the losers as a winner because of the *contrast* with the others, another easy trap for inexperienced or novice interviewers. Again, that's why you should use the candidate assessment form and have multiple interviewers with whom to compare notes.

Try to look at each candidate as a stand-alone candidate in relation to what the job requires, not in relation to other candidates. This is not always easy to do, but the first step is to just be aware of this tendency before making a final decision or judgment. A good question to ask yourself is, "If this was the only person I saw for the job, would I hire her?"

3. The "Just Like Me!" Syndrome

This one is probably obvious. As in halo or horns, this is when you like someone because he is like you. It could be where he is from, where he went to school, his style of dress, his personality style, or a host of other criteria that have little or nothing to do with his ability to do the job. Birds of a feather flock together.

Bear in mind: There are many jobs for which you need someone very different from you. For example, if you are in sales, you may judge people by their "people" skills. Are they outgoing, gregarious, and so on? If you were hiring an accountant, that could be a big mistake, especially if her job is performed in relative isolation.

In reality, you might be looking for someone who may be more reserved, introspective, and more task- and detail-oriented than relationship-oriented. Again, that's why you need to prepare for every interview and have your questions tailored to both the candidate and the job. We'll talk more about job-person matching in Chapter 6, "Assessment."

4. 80/20 Rule

See "Best Practices in Conducting the Interview"—you should be speaking only 20 percent of the time, and the candidate should be speaking 80 percent of the time.

5. Primacy/Recency

These are psychological terms for "What happened first?" and "What happened last?" We tend to remember the first thing we saw and experienced and the last thing we saw and experienced more than the muck in the middle.

Use the sales process as an analogy. A powerful "meet and greet" and "final send-off" can sometimes overshadow a less-than-stellar process in the middle. The same can hold true if a candidate has a powerful handshake, eye contact, smile, and ability to establish common ground. In other words, she makes a great first impression.

That's great, but pay as much attention to what goes on after that and don't let the first and last(ing) impression overshadow the rest of the interview.

RED FLAGS AND WARNING SIGNS

Although the interview and other screening tools are the key factors that we should use in making our hiring decisions, bear in mind that there are other factors that can also weigh for or against a candidate's hireability.

Also, the interview does not start when you begin asking the candidate questions in your office. It starts when he picks up the phone to call you and continues when he gets out of his car in the parking lot, when he greets (or doesn't greet) your receptionist or other staff, and throughout the entire process of interactions.

Here are some red flags and warning signs:

1. *Arriving late for the interview.* This should be obvious, but unless there was an act of God preventing the applicant from being on time, why in the world would you expect her to come to work on time?

2. *Treating your staff dismissively or disrespectfully.* Remember the good old days when we had secretaries? Mine was also the receptionist in the employment of-

fice. Wanda would bring the person's application and résumé to me for review while he was sitting in the reception area.

All she would have to do was let out a sigh and a look of disgust when she laid the paperwork on my desk, which then elicited a "What's wrong, Wanda?" from me. At which point, she would say, "Oh, nothing. He's just a little arrogant" or something of that nature.

This is a case where the "horns" effect is valid. If the candidate treats my secretary with disrespect before he is even hired, how do you think he is going to behave on the job? This is when he should be on his *best* behavior!

3. *Not wearing appropriate attire for the position.* This is a variable. A janitor applicant might be acceptable in clean jeans and a T-shirt, although dressing up a bit would be a plus, whereas someone applying for a management position should be wearing proper business attire. Again, it's a sign of judgment and awareness.

A good rule of thumb is, "Dress for the next job you want, not the one you have." In other words, wear aspirational attire!

4. *Meet and greet.* Did the person extend a confident handshake, look you in the eyes, smile, and greet you? This goes for both men and women. Even a cold, clammy handshake is better than no handshake at all. Again, this indicates judgment and confidence. *Note: Some cultures deems eye contact and hand-shaking inappropriate.*

5. *Talking too much.* Even though we have been stressing the 80/20 rule, there are times when a candidate goes overboard or over limits, particularly when she lacks the judgment to know when to shut up or what not to share. This usually happens when you are using open-ended questions and/or clarifying statements.

6. *Speaking negatively about past employers and experiences.* Even though the story might be true, this is an indication of the applicant's not taking responsibility for his own actions, or at least sharing what he learned from the experience, instead of placing blame on others for everything. Remember that in "Gut Wrenchers," we said to keep all responses positive and job-related?

7. *Asking about money too soon.* Granted, we all work for pay. However, good judgment says this should not be one of the first questions a candidate voices. It

shows a lack of concern of the employer's needs and priorities, demonstrates short-term, self-centered thinking, and is just poor form.

8. *Showing up unprepared.* This could include not bringing a pen and paper, not having her résumé with her, knowing nothing about the organization, and other such omissions. If someone approaches a job interview by the seat of her pants, it's a pretty sure bet that she will approach her job the same way.

9. *Using inappropriate language.* Even if your culture is laid back and informal, it never justifies a candidate's use of vulgarity or inappropriate language. Again, this is an indication of a lack of class, self-awareness, and self-monitoring. If he is that willing to let his guard down in a job interview, can you imagine what will happen with customers and coworkers?

10. *Being vague in her responses.* A key purpose of a job interview is to delve into the details of the candidate's qualifications, that is, beyond the résumé. If she is vague, nonresponsive, or evasive in her responses, even when you use the questioning techniques referred to herein, then either she has something to hide or she is just unable to articulate her thoughts. Either way, it's no way!

11. *Exhibiting poor body language.* Yes, body language is a legitimate barometer. Beyond the meet and greet, handshake, eye contact, and smile, if the candidate slumps in his chair, or even puts his feet up, that's a sign. He is on stage.

A candidate should have decent posture and demonstrate that he is alert and attentive (or at least awake!) by sitting up or, even better, sitting on the edge of his seat. Leaning back, folding his arms in front of him, and other such behavior indicates closed-mindedness, or at least defensiveness, lack of confidence and/or lack of attentiveness, and maybe even arrogance. Whatever it is, it isn't a good sign.

12. *Not asking any questions.* Remember that in the interview setup, we said to let the candidate know that she can ask you questions at the end? When you are done asking your questions, you ask the candidate what questions she has. If she has none, or if she just asks what the job pays, then this could be a red flag. It demonstrates a lack of depth of thinking, lack of understanding of or interest in a job or an organization, or a lack of preparation, and it is also somewhat insulting to you as an employer. (See the next section, "Interviewing the Interviewer.")

INTERVIEWING THE INTERVIEWER

So, you've asked all the gut-wrenching questions, and now you say, "Do you have any questions for me?" Uh-oh! Now what does the applicant do? Does he just squirm and say, "Oh, nothing." Does he just make something up on the spot?

Here's an idea! What do you think every candidate should *want* to know about your organization and her future job? Instead of just winging it, she should want to get some valuable insights. Here are some sample questions that we train people who are in career transition to use.

Why Is the Position Vacant?

What do you think this will tell the candidate? Well, would it make a difference if the last three people who held the job were fired? Or if the last three people quit after less than a year? Hmm. Could be a red flag!

Or, what if the position was just newly created? This is usually a good sign, since there is no track record to follow, it indicates growth, and it may even allow the candidate to invent his own job to some degree.

Or, what if the last person was promoted? That says that this position can lead to bigger and better things, hopefully.

Or, what if the last person retired from the position after serving in it for 30 years? That could be pretty much the opposite of the previous example. It doesn't look like there's much opportunity for advancement there! Or, conversely, it may show that there is a lot of loyalty and stability at this organization. So, as you can see, this one little question can open myriad possibilities.

What Do You See as the Biggest Challenge Facing Whoever Is in This Position in the Next Year?

This is a question to gauge the potential challenges that the candidate will be facing. It also gives her a reading on her future boss's perspectives on the position. Don't be surprised if you cannot answer this question easily, which could actually be a good thing, in a way. If the candidate makes you think, it shows that she is also thinking. By the same token, if you haven't thought about this already, your answer will probably be a candid one, that is, unscripted.

What Will Be Different a Year From Now if the Person in This Job Is Successful?

Like the previous question, this is a way for the candidate to determine your future priorities and objectives. It also tells him what he is going to need to do to be successful. He can't lose on this question. It shows concern, insight, and empathy for the boss's priorities, while getting valuable information on success factors before he makes a decision.

How Would You Describe Your Organization's Culture?

This one is pretty obvious. It's not something that a candidate can pick up in an annual report or a brochure. And yes, you can sense some of it by observation, but it's even better to hear it from the horse's mouth. Most organization loyalists are eager to recite their insider's knowledge of the organization's culture.

Again, it not only gives the candidate valuable information, but it also allows the interviewer to "show off" a little bit. That's a win-win question. (This is where the "Why Work Here?" statement comes in handy.)

As you can see, there are plenty of questions that candidates not only should ask, but also should *want* to ask. They don't need to be trivial, trite, or generic. This is their opportunity to interview you, while hopefully impressing you at the same time, and getting some real insights that they cannot get anywhere else.

CHAPTER 5

Assessment

MATCHING PEOPLE TO JOBS—BEHAVIORAL ASSESSMENT

So, you've done everything right so far! Congratulations! But, how do you measure "the right stuff" that you cannot ascertain from a résumé or an interview? Like what? Like personality style, problem-solving style, delegating style, conflict resolution style, results orientation, and many other such things.

We've discussed the use of behavioral interviewing questions at some length, but even the best and most skilled interviewers will agree that interviewing is as much an art as it is a science. It has even been said that interviews can be one of the least reliable and valid steps in the recruitment and selection process.

The most successful organizations and those that always get the pick of the litter also have some interesting hiring philosophies, such as:

Hire hard, manage easy

Hire slow, fire fast

Hire for style, train for skills

These three philosophies have some things in common, most particularly spending more time and effort on the front end (screening and selection) so that less time and effort are required later in performance management, training, coaching, discipline, and ultimately termination or resignation.

Organizations that do *not* practice these philosophies are usually of the ilk that thinks, "If we don't do it right, we can always do it over." It is sadly ironic that some organizations look at what is being advocated in this kit as being too time-consuming. But instead, they waste tons more time using a hit-and-miss, revolving-door approach and end up taking more time to do it wrong, while constantly dealing with poor performance and high turnover. That's a lose-lose-lose.

Hire Hard, Manage Easy

Hire hard, manage easy involves just that. What's in it for you, the manager, is to make your life easier and better by not having to micromanage and be burdened every day with dealing with people who cannot perform at the level necessary for you to do your job. If all you do is manage, you can never lead.

Imagine what your life would be like if you could put your people on autopilot and not be haunted by whether they are performing or not. You could actually go on vacation!

Although this is a hiring *philosophy*, in practice it involves just about everything you are learning in this kit, especially the behavioral profiling and interviewing processes. Yes, it takes more time and effort up front, but it saves you a great deal of time and effort later because you have the right person doing the right job, hopefully for a long time.

Hire Slow, Fire Fast

This is almost a carbon copy of hire hard, manage easy, but it emphasizes both ends of the employment cycle. In other words, if we hire hard and hire slow, we probably won't have to do a lot of firing. However, even using all of the tools and techniques in this kit, there will still be occasions when, for whatever reason, the person we hire is just not a fit.

Obviously, we give people the tools, training, and time to turn their performance around, but given all the work that was done on the front end of the hiring process, this does not need to take forever. Once we have determined that we and they have made a mistake and that they are in either the wrong job or the wrong organization, it helps no one to have them linger on.

Cut your losses and theirs. We are not saying that you should be cold and callous, but the really compassionate thing to do is to part ways so that both parties can move on and be successful.

Hire for Style, Train for Skills

The first two philosophies are exactly what we are advocating and teaching you in this kit: using job descriptions, preparation, résumé analysis, targeted and in-depth behavioral interviewing, and so on. However, the third philosophy, hire for style, train for skills (borrowed from Southwest Airlines), adds another critical component.

The average employer (which is what you *don't* want to be) places too much emphasis on skills rather than on style. In other words, it assumes that if you flew an airplane at another airline, then you can probably fly one at ours. Duuh.

The hire for style, train for skills model says, "I can train you on our processes. I can train you on our product or service. But I can't train you to connect with people, or to interact positively with negative people, or to have a natural sense of humor!"

In other words, it is easier to train someone on a skill (a process, filling out forms, using a software program, and so on) than it is to change his natural personality style. If you think you can change someone's personality, then you obviously have never been married. And that's someone whom you love, and whom you have your entire life to work on! As we said in the preface, you can't teach a pig to sing; you also can't teach a rock to swim.

So, how do we assess whether someone's style is a good match for a particular job? Well, first you have to know what the job requires, beyond skills (e.g., communication style, problem-solving style, stress behaviors, delegating style, coaching style, and so forth). These are things that even the most skilled interviewer cannot adequately assess from an interview alone, because any savvy candidate can either lie or fake it for an hour.

This requires a formal, valid psychological profiling instrument that is correlated to the actual job. The one we recommend is the Role Behavior Analysis (RBA) combined with the Personal Profile System (PPS). These tools are the most cost-effective and job-effective systems available today.

Without trying to make you a guru on psychological assessments, here is the quick and dirty explanation. You profile a job using one or more Role Behavior Analyses to identify those behaviors that are needed to provide the best fit for the particular job. This can be done by the supervisor, by a top-performing incumbent, or even by both. Believe it or not, it takes only a matter of minutes, and you only have to do it once, unless the job changes dramatically.

The reason this instrument uses the term *role* instead of *job* is that most jobs involve multiple roles. For example, one day I might be writing this book, which requires being alone and focused on creating and developing concepts and then putting them into words. The next day, I might be in front of an audience presenting these concepts, which requires a very different type of behavior, that is, interacting, speaking, and influencing.

If we were profiling my job, as just described, we might have two RBAs because those two very different behaviors take up a large percentage of my average day or week. It doesn't make a lot of sense to profile too many roles, because the person may be performing some of them for only a very small percentage of the time, and most people can adapt for short periods.

Once you have a consensus on the ideal profile, you merely save it on your computer, and whenever you have a candidate whom you are seriously considering hiring, you have her complete a Personal Profile, which should not take more than 15 to 20 minutes.

The computer software automatically generates a comparison of the RBA with the PPS and identifies where the candidate's style is a "good fit," where it is a "stretch," or where he may have to "redirect" his energy to adapt.

A good fit is exactly that. The candidate has the exact style that the job requires. For example, my interactive style fits well with the role of speaking, training, and presenting to groups.

A stretch means that the candidate is going to have to be something that she is not. For example, I am not a detail person, but I can do it. However, if you put me in a cubicle for eight hours a day, every day, doing data entry and analysis, I would go crazy. I may have the ability (skill), but I do not have the personality (style). Therefore, it would be a stretch for me to do it. Again, please note that this is an issue only if the stretch role makes up a large portion of the person's job.

Finally, a "redirect" means that the candidate has too much of something. Using the same example, I may be too outgoing and needing of interaction to be stuck in a cubicle doing data entry and analysis. Therefore, I would need to redirect the energy that would normally go into my interacting with others, and use it to focus on data entry and analysis.

To see what these reports look like, go to the Recruitment Folder on your CD.

Also note the Performance Coaching Questions at the end of the form, which can be used as interview questions for job candidates or as coaching questions for members of your current staff. This process is just as powerful for current employee performance coaching as it is for screening and selection.

In order to implement one of these systems, initially you would need the assistance of a professional who is certified in these instruments to train you and your team on how to use them. Please feel free to contact the authors of this kit for more information and guidance on this process.

It isn't rocket science, but there are some clear dos and don'ts. For example, never call one of these instruments a test. In Equal Employment Opportunity verbiage, that implies that one can either pass or fail the instrument, which is not the case. There is no right or wrong, good or bad answer, and therefore these instruments are among many inputs into the hiring decision.

After using these instruments enough times, you will become more and more proficient at being able to read the reports and be able to make much better hiring decisions, without the ongoing need for an outside consultant.

If you still aren't sold on the idea that matching the person and the job is critical to your and their success, consider the *Harvard Business Review* study in Figure 5–1.

What does this study say? To sum up, it says that those organizations that follow the hiring practices recommended herein will see their retention (employee loyalty) rate *at least* double, and possibly as much as quintuple (be five times better), compared to those who do not ensure that there is a good match between the person and the job.

So, if these practices allow you to both reduce turnover *and* elicit higher performance, the math becomes pretty easy and obvious. The average cost to replace

FIGURE 5-1. JOB MATCH OR NO JOB MATCH

Job Match?

High Turnover Industry – Sample Size: 13,102

	No	Yes
Percentage who quit or were fired after 6 months:	46%	24%
Percentage who quit or were fired after 14 months:	57%	28%

Job Match?

Low Turnover Industry – Sample Size: 5,941

	No	Yes
Percentage who quit or were fired after 6 months:	25%	5%
Percentage who quit or were fired after 14 months:	34%	8%

Source: Herbert M. Greenberg and Jeanne Greenberg, "Job Matching for Better Sales Performance," *Harvard Business Review*, Vol. 58, No. 5.

just one $40,000 employee has been proven to be at least $50,000, and that's just the hard, tangible cost.

Factor in the lack of stability, impact on customer satisfaction, impact on those who have to pick up the slack, need for retraining, and hassle for you, and the cost-benefit becomes a no-brainer. Go back to the cost of turnover worksheet in the Introduction.

To quote directly from the *Harvard Business Review* study, "It's not just experience, or college degrees or other accepted factors; success hinges on a fit with the job."

USING THE CANDIDATE ASSESSMENT FORM

As soon as the interviews are over (yes, that's plural—at least three people should be interviewing each candidate, remember?), you need to document your findings in a legal and consistent format.

Following the same format you used in the candidate interview worksheet, you will now translate your notes and findings into a scoring system so that you can compare them with those of the other interviewers immediately, while everything is fresh in your minds.

You will discover both consensus and conflict, which is good, because it generates dialogue and analysis, and ultimately results in better hiring decisions. In the event that you find yourself wildly opposed to another interviewer's rating(s), go back to the job description and Role Behavior Analysis and determine if they are still valid, or if you may be measuring the wrong thing.

Generally, when all the interviewers know what they are looking for, there is more consensus than conflict. That's why you did all of the preparatory work beforehand. Regardless, this process focuses the discussions and decision making on preestablished, job-related criteria, which not only keeps you legal, but improves the quality of your hiring.

The Candidate Assessment Form is given on the next page; it also appears on the enclosed CD.

Candidate Assessment Form

Position: _____

Candidate: _____

Interviewed By: _____   Date: _____

Candidate Assessment Rating:

1 = Unacceptable   2 = Below Average   3 = Acceptable   4 = Above Average   5 = Excellent

Category	Notes	Candidate Rating				
Presentation and manner		1	2	3	4	5
Experience/work history		1	2	3	4	5
Education and training		1	2	3	4	5
Skills and knowledge		1	2	3	4	5
Personality		1	2	3	4	5
Communication skills		1	2	3	4	5

CHAPTER 6

Reference Checking

One of the most important steps in the employment process is the proper vetting of candidates. Surprisingly, more than 75 percent of employers do not conduct reference or background checks of their potential candidates. Done properly, this one final process can save you a significant amount of time, management, and money. Remember what we said earlier: The cost of a bad hire is more than the cost per hire. In certain roles and in smaller companies, a bad hire can cost you your company.

Before conducting reference checks or background investigations, you must have the candidate's written permission. This is easily accomplished by having the following release statement at the end of your application for employment.

Applicant Information Release

I hereby authorize any person, educational institution, or company I have listed as a reference on my employment application to disclose in good faith any information they may have regarding my qualifications and fitness for employment. I will hold [Your Business], any former employers or educational institutions, and any other persons giving references free of liability for the exchange of this information and any other reasonable and necessary information incident to the employment process.

Signed: _____   Date: _____

You may run into an employer who won't tell you anything more than "name, rank, and serial number" information for fear that the employee may sue. If you run into that, remind the employer that most states consider the information "qualifiedly privileged." That means that the information is protected, and that the employer who shares it is protected unless the information is given:

> With known falsity
> In bad faith
> With reckless disregard for the truth

Sometimes you can get more information from coworkers or supervisors, but often they too are instructed not to discuss why the employee left or if the employee would be rehired. A number of states *require* former employers to provide a job reference letter or some information about people who worked for them. No matter what, document whatever information you do get and note who gave it to you. Also note the information that others would *not* give you.

Another compelling reason to conduct thorough reference checking and background investigations is to reduce the risk of a "negligent hiring" lawsuit.

NEGLIGENT HIRING—WHAT IS IT?

In order for a customer, employee, or other third party to prevail in a negligent hiring suit against an employer, the following must generally be shown:

> The existence of an employment relationship between the employer and the worker
> The employee's unfitness
> The employer's actual or constructive knowledge of the employee's unfitness (failure to investigate can lead to a finding of constructive knowledge)
> The employee's act or omission causing the third party's injuries
> The employer's negligence in hiring the employee as the most likely cause of the plaintiff's injuries

If you are ever served with a negligent hiring lawsuit, the first step you should take is to call your lawyer. In fact, that's the first step you should take any time you receive legal papers. But it's especially important that you call a lawyer immediately when you're sued because you have a certain number of days in which to file an answer to the lawsuit.

The number of days that you have will vary depending upon where the suit was filed, but you could have as little as two weeks to respond. If you are served with legal documents and you don't have a lawyer, you should find one right away. Once you have a lawyer, he can tell you more about your chances of winning or losing the lawsuit.

REFERENCE CHECK PROCESS

1. Identify yourself immediately, explain your position with your organization, and tell the person why you are calling about the applicant.
2. Ask if the person is free to discuss the prior employment situation.
3. Assure your contact that any discussion you have will be held in confidence.
4. Tell the person about the position for which the applicant is being considered, so that she can give a more accurate evaluation of the applicant.
5. After giving background information on the position that you want to fill, ask a general response question, such as, "How do you think the applicant would fit into our position?" After the person responds, ask more specific questions.
6. Let the person talk freely for as long as he wishes without interruption. Often a question from you at the wrong time will shut off further information.
7. Follow up and ask more questions when the contact is reluctant to discuss certain areas. Many times a further explanation of why you are digging will get you the information you want.
8. Watch for obvious pauses in answering when you ask questions. Often this may be a sign that further questions may bring more information that you might not otherwise receive.
9. Do not hang up until you are sure that you know the opinion of the person you have called. Often you will receive ambiguous answers. The person

called may give very little useful information. A technique that frequently works is to summarize the conversation by making either of the following two statements: "I take it that you don't recommend the applicant very highly for the position" or "I take it that you recommend the applicant very highly for the position." Sometimes this brings the responses that you need.

10. Glance at your checklist of questions to be sure that you've covered everything.

11. Always end the call by asking the person, "Would you rehire the applicant?" Often this question brings forth information that you were unable to get by other questions.

12. Be sure to thank your contact for her help.

REFERENCE CHECK QUESTIONS

Basic Reference Check Sample Questions

- What were the beginning and ending employment dates for this individual?
- What was this individual's beginning and ending salary?
- What positions did the individual hold?
- Did this individual earn promotions?
- What were the individual's most recent job duties?
- Why did the individual leave your company?
- Is there any reason why your company would not rehire this individual?
- Would you recommend this individual for a position at another company? Why or why not?
- How did this individual's performance compare to that of other employees with similar job duties?
- In your opinion, what are the individual's strengths? Weaknesses?
- Did this individual get along well with management and peers?
- Was this individual a team player?
- Was this individual a motivated self-starter?
- Did any personal problems affect this individual's work performance?

➤ Do you think this individual will perform well as a [job title]?

➤ What kind of job is best suited for this individual's abilities?

➤ How would you describe the individual's overall performance?

➤ Is there anything of significance that you'd like to add?

Additional Reference Check Sample Questions for Management-Level Employees

➤ How would you describe the individual's leadership, managerial, or supervisory skills?

➤ Does the individual communicate well, both orally and in writing?

➤ How do you rate the individual's ability to plan short term? Long term?

➤ Did the individual make sound and timely decisions?

➤ Did the individual get along well with management, subordinates, and peers?

➤ Did the individual plan, administer, and make budget well?

➤ How would you describe the individual's technical skills?

➤ Did the individual demonstrate honesty and integrity?

➤ How well did the individual manage crisis, pressure, or stress?

➤ Describe the individual's ability to attract and counsel top talent.

CHAPTER 7

Drug Testing

INFORMATION ON DRUG TESTING IN THE WORKPLACE

Workers who are impaired by illegal drugs can threaten the safety and productivity of a business and could even cause legal problems for the business. Although employers have the legal right to insist on a drug-free workplace, enforcing that right can be a contentious issue. Any steps you take to maintain a drug-free workplace must respect the workers' legal rights to privacy and nondiscrimination.

Many employers, especially small business owners, rely on interviews and background checks to identify drug users. Many drug users are proficient at hiding their drug habits, however, and easily breeze through interviews and background checks. That is why some firms choose to test workers' urine samples or hair follicles for drugs. But before you implement such a policy, make sure that you understand how the law governs drug testing.

Federal Law

Drug testing falls under the Americans with Disabilities Act (ADA), which includes several key features:

> ➤ The ADA makes it illegal for any employer to test a prospective employee without first making a conditional offer of employment.
> ➤ The ADA also says that you cannot discriminate against prospective employees on the basis of past drug-related problems. Then again, you may refuse to hire

people if you have reason to believe that they will return to substance abuse or endanger the safety and health of your workers. If you are not sure how to proceed with an applicant who has a history of drug abuse, consult an attorney. The ADA does not prohibit asking a person with a history of substance abuse to enroll in a rehabilitation program before joining your firm.

State Laws

Laws vary from state to state and change frequently. You can find out the details of your state's drug testing laws by contacting a trade organization, your state government, or an employment lawyer. Your right to test workers for drug use depends on several factors:

➤ *The job itself.* If a job has the potential to place the employee, coworkers, or the public in danger, there may be stronger legal justification to test for drugs.

➤ *Evidence of a drug problem.* Some states require you to show probable cause to suspect that employees are impaired before testing them for drugs.

➤ *Whether the worker is already on staff.* Once applicants have been hired, your rights to test them for drug use may diminish. Some states require visible evidence of substance abuse, such as an accident, a visible decline in work quality, or the discovery of illicit drugs in the workplace, before you have the legal right to test an employee. Testing current employees at random or without prior notice is also illegal in many states.

KINDS OF DRUG TESTING

Employment Contingent on Successful Drug Test

As an employer, you can require an applicant to complete a drug test successfully before being hired. Preemployment substance testing should be used to screen all applicants for certain positions or for all positions.

Organizations may want to test all new hires, particularly if they have a drug-free workplace or have another type of test schedule in place. Alternatively, they may want to test only those hired for hazardous or high-risk positions.

Employers need to remember that any time a group is singled out for any reason, particularly a reason as controversial as substance testing, concerns about discriminatory practices can arise.

Random Drug Test

Random substance testing is testing of employees on an irregular, unannounced schedule. The use of random testing is critical if employers are serious about addressing the illegal use of drugs and alcohol in the workplace. This method is the only way to carry out nondiscriminatory, nonselective substance testing, and it is the only way to detect casual substance abusers in the organization.

If a company is going to have a meaningful substance-testing program, a random test is the most critical component of that program. Employers can lessen their risk if they ensure that the tests are truly random. Using a random-number-generating computer program so that the selection of employees for testing is not influenced by human decisions can do this.

For Cause—Reasonable Suspicion Testing

Testing employees who are suspected of substance abuse on the job can take several forms. Employers can test employees who behave erratically, smell of alcohol, or are the subject of complaints from the public or other employees. Employers can also routinely conduct a substance test after any employment-related accident.

Department of Transportation and Drug Testing

Many workers are covered by the Department of Transportation (DOT) Regulations, including mass transit workers (Federal Transit Administration); motor carrier workers, primarily truck drivers with a commercial driver's license (Federal Highway Administration); aviation workers (Federal Aviation Administration); railroad workers (Federal Railroad Administration); marine workers (Merchant Marine covered by

Coast Guard regulations); and natural gas and pipeline workers (Research and Special Programs Administration).

The regulations also include maintenance personnel, dispatchers, and security guards who carry firearms in these operations.

Employees covered by these regulations must be tested for alcohol, marijuana, cocaine, opiates, phencyclidine, and amphetamines. The regulations require uniform testing standards. They include a very complex series of testing and documenting procedures, along with employee notice, retest, and confidentiality requirements. The procedures outlined in the Department of Transportation (DOT) regulations can be used as a good framework for establishing a drug-testing program.

Drug Testing Policy

Prior to Employment at [Company Name]

[Company Name] requires that applicants for employment report to the clinic or medical office specified by [Company Name] for drug testing *prior* to employment by the company. Costs of the tests will be borne by [Company Name]. [Company Name] reserves the right to reject an applicant if the test indicates the use of illegal controlled substances.

Testing Employees

[Company Name] may require a drug test of a regular employee or trainee in the following situations:

1. For reasonable suspicion
2. After accidents
3. After medical or drug-abuse treatment

[Company Name] also reserves the right to require that an employee who fails a drug test undertake a company-sponsored rehabilitation program at a facility approved by [Company Name] and at the employee's expense and without pay by the employer as a condition for continuing in the workplace. Further, pending completion of such program, the employee may be removed from tasks that may endanger the quality of work or the safety of the employee or coworkers.

Substance Abuse Policy Acknowledgment/Release

I hereby consent to submit to urinalysis and/or other tests as shall be determined/required by [Company Name], the "Company," for the purpose of determining any drug and/or alcohol content thereof.

I agree that [Enter Laboratory Name] (a certified lab) or other designated collection site may collect these specimens for these tests and may test them or forward them for analysis to a certified testing laboratory designated by the Company.

I further agree to and hereby authorize the release of the results of said tests to an authorized medical review officer (MRO), the Company, or an authorized agent of the Company.

I understand that it is the current, illegal use of drugs and/or abuse of alcohol that would prohibit me from being employed at this Company. Applicants for employment and employees can be tested for the use of illegal drugs and alcohol.

I further agree to hold harmless the Company and its agents (including the above-named laboratory and the collection site) from any liability arising in whole or in part out of the collection of specimens, testing, and use of the information from said testing in connection with the Company's consideration of my employment, or my employment application if a candidate for employment.

I further agree that a reproduced copy of this consent and release form shall have the same force and effect as the original.

I also hereby certify that I have received and read the Substance Abuse Policy Statement and have had the drug-free workplace program explained to me. I understand that if my performance indicates that it is necessary, I will submit to a drug and/or alcohol test. I also understand that failure to comply with a drug and/or alcohol testing request or a confirmed positive result for the illegal use of drugs and/or alcohol will lead to discipline up to and including termination of employment and/or forfeiture of workers' compensation benefits.

I have carefully read the foregoing and fully understand its contents.

Applicant/Employee:

Print Name: _____ Soc. Sec. No. _____ — _____ — _____

Signature: _____ Date: _____

Witness Printed Name: _____

Witness Signature: _____

This form will become part of an employee's personnel file.

CHAPTER 8

Immigration

I-9 FORM—EMPLOYMENT ELIGIBILITY VERIFICATION

This form must be completed for all employees, whether citizens or noncitizens, hired after November 6, 1986, in order to show evidence of the employee's eligibility to work in the United States according to the Immigration and Naturalization Service (INS).

The employee completes Section 1 of the form and provides documents to establish his identity and employment eligibility.

The employer reviews the documents to ensure that they are acceptable and signs the certification part, Section 2, on Form I-9. Copies of the documents reviewed must be stapled to the I-9 form and routed through the same channels as the new hire paperwork. Copies of identification cards such as a driver's license and a social security card must be made for record purposes.

Do *not* send this form to the Immigration and Naturalization Service. Employers must retain the completed form.

Retain the I-9 form for each employee either for three years after the date of hire or for one year after employment is terminated, whichever is later.

Make the I-9 form available for inspection to an officer of the INS, the Department of Labor (DOL), upon request. You can find a copy of the latest I-9 form on the Immigration and Naturalization Service web site, http://www.ins.usdoj.gov/graphics/formsfee/forms/files/i-9.pdf.

TYPES OF U.S. VISAS

(B-1) Visa Waiver Program

U.S. employees can go into certain countries (e.g., the UK) for up to 90 days for business. Only a passport is needed.

(F-1) Practical Training

An immigrant student is allowed to be in the United States for up to one year after college. The individual must file for an Employment Authorization Card for I-9 purposes. This card takes about three months to receive. The student must receive it from her or his college or university. The work that the student performs for an employer must be done in the same field of study as his or her degree.

H-1B Visa Requirements

The H-1B is a special occupational visa.

The candidate must have at least a Bachelor of Arts degree. However, under *Option B*, academic background and employment experience can be combined to equal the BA status for an H-1B visa.

The employer needs to tell the Credential Evaluator (CE) what the company is looking for. The CE will try to equate your needs to the appropriate credentials accurately.

Filling a Position That Requires a BA. The *Dictionary of Occupational Titles* (DOT) lists all jobs and educational levels. The specific vocational preparation (SVP) number lets you know how much education is required for a particular position.

A prevailing wage quote is required. The Labor Condition Application (LCA) declares to the INS authorities that the wage you are offering is equal to the wage that other people with that specific skill set in that geographic area are being paid. The wage that the employer is offering must be at least 95 percent of the prevailing wage.

A State Employment Security Agency (SESA) request is a request for that prevailing wage from the Department of Labor.

An alternative to requesting the prevailing wage is to review surveys of wages in local markets in that geographic region. This is not the easiest procedure to back up if you are audited.

Labor Condition Application (LCA) Form. The Labor Condition Application (LCA) form needs to be submitted before the employer files for an H-1B. It is supposed to take 24 to 48 hours for an LCA to become active, but it can take up to two weeks.

An LCA is needed both for a new hire and for a move within the company. You do not need a new LCA if an employee moves to a similar position. However, for the holder of an H-1B visa to work in a new site or location within the same company, the LCA needs to be refiled. For example:

To move from software engineer to senior software engineer, no new LCA is needed.

To move from a sales position to an IT position, a new LCA is needed.

The LCA form is job-specific. If the job changes, you must reapply. Therefore, you want to define the duties broadly and the requirements tightly.

H-1B-Dependent Employers. These are companies where at least 15 percent of the employees are H-1B holders.

There are three options that employers may attest to on the bottom of the LCA form:

- We are an H-1B Dependent Employer.
- We are not an H-1B Dependent Employer.
- We are an H-1B Dependent Employer, but this form applies only to H-1B exempt positions (i.e., the employee was paid at least $60,000 a year or has a master's degree).

All H-1B employers must have the following in their public access file:

- A copy of the LCA form
- Documentation of the prevailing wage
- Documentation showing that the employee received a copy of the LCA (a letter to the employee)
- Documentation regarding the actual wage paid to the employee (i.e., the internal salary scale and grading system)

H-1B Process

- File the LCA before filing for the H-1B.
- File the H-1B petition. Get a credentials evaluation, which costs about $75.
- Send the H-1B to the local service center.

If an employee has an H-1B and goes to another company, he can work once the second H-1B is filed.

An H-1B can be denied for the following reasons:

- Educational background
- Company standing (e.g., start-ups may be too risky to support H-1B employees)

Issues With H-1B:

- An H-1B takes approximately three months to get.
- The cost is about $1,110 per H-1B.
- An H-1B is good for three years plus a three-year extension, for a total of six years.
- The United States accepts only 115,000 H-1B applicants per year, although this number can change. For example, a law passed effective October 1, 2000,

increased the number to 195,000 H-1B applicants accepted per year for the next three years. Please note that this follows the U.S. federal government fiscal calendar, which starts October 1 of each year. The available visas usually run out by March or April.

H-1B Alternatives

➤ *(B-1) H-1B Waivers.* U.S. employees can go into certain countries (e.g., the UK) for up to 90 days for business. Only a passport is needed.

➤ *(F-1) Practical Training.* An immigrant student is allowed to be in the United States for a total of one year after college.

➤ *TN (Trade NAFTA).* This is a program for Canadian and Mexican citizens. The cost is $50 or $55. An individual cannot get a TN visa if the applicant is in the green card process. However, an individual can get a TN visa if the applicant has an H-1B in process.

For Canadians, the following conditions apply:

➤ No LCA is required.
➤ The holder must be a Canadian citizen.
➤ There is a strict list of occupations for which TN visas are allowed. Only 63 occupations qualify. (The employer needs to fit its job description into one of these 63 occupations.)
➤ The visa holder's original diploma must be presented at the port of entry.
➤ The TN is a temporary visa. It can be used for two or three years, then it must be switched to an H-1B.

If a Canadian's TN visa application is denied, the employer and its lawyer have the right to talk to the examiner. If a Canadian applicant for a TN visa is denied entry to the United States, he or she should not try to enter the United States at other locations. The person has been entered into the system, and this will show up if he or she tries to enter at other checkpoints.

The TN visa program is not the best choice when dealing with Mexican citizens. However, for Mexicans, the following conditions apply:

- You are required to go through the H-1B process.
- You need to file an LCA and a TN.
- It takes three months to get a TN.
- A TN is authorized for one year.

L-1 Visa (Intracompany Transfers)

This is a program allowing employees of foreign companies with offices in the United States to bring foreign employees to their U.S. operations. For example, Bayer uses this program frequently, as the company has headquarters in both Pittsburgh and Germany. The following restrictions apply:

- There must be a qualifying relationship between the foreign employee and the employer.
- The employee must have worked for the foreign company for one year out of the past three years.
- The employee has to be a member of executive management or have specialized knowledge (technology that is unique to the company).
- The individual must be filling a similar position in the U.S. company:
  - An L-1A is specific to executive managers and lasts for seven years.
  - An L-1B is specific to specialized knowledge workers, takes four to six weeks to be active, and lasts for five years.
- The fastest way to process either of these is through a Blanket L status, which avoids filing petitions with the INS. The individual and the request are sent directly to the U.S. Consulate overseas. The request takes three to five days to process.

Green Card Process

A *Labor Certification* showing the Department of Labor that hiring a full-time foreigner is not taking a job away from qualified, interested U.S. workers is needed.

The employer cannot require any skills or credentials that are not a business necessity. Candidates must meet all of the qualifications before they can work for your company.

The employer must run a blind ad in a newspaper or trade journal for three consecutive days, including a Sunday.

The employer must post the job in the workplace. The salary range must be on the posting. (This can be the prospective pay; it does not have to be what you are paying for the position right now.) The bottom number of the range must be at least 95 percent of the prevailing wage. The job title and job description must also be on the posting.

There is a 30-day recruitment period.

The employer must review all résumés, then contact all qualified candidates, go over their qualifications, and document this. Send a certified letter if you cannot get in touch with a candidate.

Submit a recruitment summary. This should include:

➤ A letter summarizing what you did
➤ Actual ads (tear sheets)
➤ The internal posting, as well as where and when you posted it
➤ Copies of résumés received

Chart the candidate requirements.

You must supply notes on each step and each process if you are audited.

If there are enough qualified and interested U.S. workers, you must withdraw the green card application and try again.

If you have multiple openings, the ad must state "multiple openings." You can do this only if you need more than one person for the same positions. You can hire one U.S. worker, and if there is not a second qualified and interested U.S. worker, then the person filling the second position can file for a green card.

A six-month trial period is allowed to make sure that the employee is a good fit before the employer starts the green card process.

Letters of agreement for voluntary termination are becoming popular with companies so that the company does not have to keep footing the cost of the green card if an employee leaves shortly after getting the green card. If an employee leaves earlier than one year after the green card becomes effective, the employer may require him to pay back some or all of the costs. For example:

> If the employee leaves after less than one year, the employee pays 100 percent of the green card costs.
> If the employee leaves after less than two years, the employee pays 50 percent of the green card costs.
> If the employee leaves after less than three years, the employee pays none of the green card costs.

I-140 Immigrant Visa Petition

The only countries that exceed their supply of U.S. visas are China and India. Chinese and Indians can apply for the second supply of U.S. visas.

An applicant for an E-B2 must have a master's degree or BA and five years' experience. The position must require a master's degree.

An applicant for an E-B3 must have a bachelor's degree. The position must require a bachelor's degree.

Form I-485, Adjustment of Status

This procedure allows an eligible applicant to become a lawful permanent resident of the United States without having to go abroad and apply for an immigrant visa. The applicant's spouse and children are eligible to file for work visas at this time.

Table 8-1 summarizes the requirements for various types of visas.

TABLE 8-1 SELECTED U.S. VISA STATUSES

This is a general summary of a complex area of law and does not constitute legal advice.
Contact your immigration attorney to discuss particular questions or cases.

Permit Category	Initial Length of Stay	Maximum Length of Stay	Can You Draw a Salary in the United States?	Other Information
B-1 Visitor for Business	Usually granted for 3 to 6 months	Up to 1 year	No, but you may be reimbursed for incidental expenses	People in this category may negotiate contracts, develop business leads, meet with colleagues, and seek employment in the United States. Apply directly to a U.S. Consulate for a visa.
B-2 Tourist	6 months	1 year initially; may be extended an additional 6 months	No, and may not be reimbursed for expenses by a U.S. source	
H-1B Specialty Occupation	Up to 3 years	6 years	Yes	A Labor Condition Application must be approved prior to filing with the INS. A needs petition must be approved by the INS.
H-2B Temporary Worker	Up to 1 year	Length of stay cannot be extended for more than 3 consecutive years	Yes	Temporary labor certification must be obtained. Each application for an extension must be accompanied by a new temporary labor certification. A needs petition must be approved by the INS.
H-3 Trainee	Up to 2 years	2 years	Yes	A structured training program must exist. Extensions are possible under the same terms that apply to admission. A needs petition must be approved by the INS.
TN-1	1 year; renewed annually	Technically none, but must be for "temporary entry," which means entry without the intent to establish permanent residence	Yes	Available only to Canadian and Mexican citizens. Canadians can apply directly at the U.S. border. Mexican TNs are treated almost exactly the same way as H-1Bs (see above). The applicant must be entering the United States to work in specifically included occupations.

TABLE 8-1 (CONTINUED)

Permit Category	Initial Length of Stay	Maximum Length of Stay	Can You Draw a Salary in the United States?	Other Information
L-1 Intracompany Transferee	3 years	7 years for managers and executives	Yes	For a start-up operation, a visa will be granted for 1 year. The employee must have worked for the foreign branch for at least 1 year out of the last 3 years prior to the transfer. A needs petition must be approved by the INS.
J-1 Exchange Visitor	12 to 18 months	5 years for specialized knowledge employees	Yes	The applicant must participate in a U.S. Immigration–approved company exchange visitor/training program. Certain J-1 visa holders are subject to a 2-year foreign residence requirement.
F-1 Foreign Student Intracompany	Duration of studies	18 months for business and industrial trainees	Only if employment is authorized in special circumstances	Employment authorization is granted only for emergencies, or where course credit for employment (practicum) is granted, or for up to one year associated with the completion of a course of studies.

CHAPTER 9

Benefits

(Please note that benefits law, regulations, and provisions are constantly changing, and that the information provided herein is intended to serve as guidelines and general information only. Please consult with a legal or certified benefits professional when making decisions about benefits, coverages, and so on.)

STANDARD BENEFITS PACKAGES

A standard benefits package generally includes some level of health coverage, a pension plan, and a few others like dental, life, short-term disability, long-term disability, and vision insurance. Keep in mind that to receive a competitive rate on health plans and to be able to participate in pension plans, a company must have at least five employees, and larger cost advantages happen over 50 employees.

Health Benefits

Companies usually offer their employees a choice between two different types of health insurances: a) an HMO (health maintenance organization) and b) a PPO (preferred provider organization). Typically, companies try to cover between 60 and 80 percent of the cost of medical insurance for employees and their dependents. Depending on the demographics of their workforce, smaller companies sometimes cover 100 percent of the health insurance cost for their employees and their families while only a few carry none for their dependents.

Dental coverage is generally included as a health benefit and follows a similar reimbursement pattern.

Vision coverage is a generous added plus. Vision plans usually include free annual eye exams plus a yearly allowance for new glasses or contact lenses.

Long-term disability insurance and life insurance are standard benefits, while short-term disability insurance isn't.

401(k) and Savings Benefits

Most companies try to put some kind of savings, IRA, or 401(k) or 403(b) (for non-profit organizations) plan in place. In addition, more established companies may consider a defined-contribution or defined-benefit program. You should consult your benefits broker for specific advice on which program is appropriate for you.

Extra Benefits and Perks

Some companies offer special programs like in-house meals or meal reimbursement for exempt employees working through dinner and sometimes daily lunches. No benefits plan is going to satisfy everyone, but companies should strive for some degree of flexibility in their overall package.

Be aware of your employee demographics when you select plans, add benefits, or make other changes. Older workers, for example, might care more about the cost of hospital stays or want greater flexibility in choosing their own doctor, whereas younger workers might be more worried about reducing their out-of-pocket expenses. A good benefits brokerage firm should be able to provide guidance on which plans to consider based on your workforce.

OFFERING HEALTH INSURANCE PLANS IS A COMPETITIVE ADVANTAGE

The quality of your benefits package can make a significant difference between attracting top candidates and average employees.

Health insurance, paid vacations, and 401(k)/pension plans are the most important component of an employee benefits package.

Health plans that are fully funded by the employer are rare today, and rising health-care costs make these plans prohibitively expensive for many business owners. Fortunately, there are some ways for even the smallest businesses to offer health benefits.

Today most employees share insurance costs. And this is an effective tool that helps employees value their health-care plans.

Be certain to have your insurance broker research your market thoroughly to make sure that you offer competitive benefits. Remember that the same types of companies compete for similar pools of employees and in times of low unemployment the slightest benefit differences can make a big difference to employees. This is particularly true in specific geographic regions where talented labor pools are drawn in numerous directions. During the dot-com rage of the 1990s the competition for labor was considered a "war for talent" in certain regions of the country, like Palo Alto (the Silicon Valley) and Austin, Texas, to name a couple.

KINDS OF HEALTH INSURANCE

There are three basic types of health insurance:

- Health maintenance organization (HMO)
- Preferred provider organization (PPO)
- Traditional indemnity plans or fee for service (FFS)

Most people with private health insurance have some form of managed care, most commonly a health maintenance organization and/or a preferred provider organization. HMOs and PPOs both involve an agreement between the insurer and a selected network of health-care providers. There are usually specific standards for selecting providers and a formal procedure to provide high-quality care.

Health Maintenance Organization

A health maintenance organization is an association of health-care professionals and medical facilities that provides the patient with a particular package of health care for a fixed amount of money paid in advance for a determined period of time.

The HMO contracts with health-care professionals and facilities to provide the determined amount of care. Generally, a patient cannot request care from any provider other than the doctors and medical facilities that are under contract with the HMO. Primary-care physicians in an HMO determine whether or not a patient needs to see a specialist. Patients do not have the right to see a specialist unless the primary-care doctor authorizes the consultation.

An employer usually pays for this care at a fixed price per employee. Employees usually do not have any significant out-of-pocket expenses with an HMO. However, the employee does not have the freedom to visit the doctors or medical facilities that he would like to visit if the doctors or medical facilities are outside the approved network. An employee also cannot get the specialized medical care that he believes is needed if his primary-care doctor does not approve the idea of visiting a specialist.

Preferred Provider Organization

A PPO has arrangements with health-care professionals and medical facilities that have agreed to accept lower fees from the patient for their services. Network health-care providers make referrals, but plan members can self-refer to doctors and specialists, including those outside the plan.

Participants who visit network doctors pay copayments, or set amounts for specific services; individuals who go to health-care professionals and/or medical facilities outside the network pay higher fees in the form of deductibles and copayments. PPO members also are required to make up the difference between what their personal provider charges and what the health-care plan pays.

There is typically a wider variety of choices in a PPO than in an HMO, and the plan is therefore more costly. Participants usually have the right to obtain services outside of those provided by the PPO, but they are then obligated to pay a greater percentage of the fee for services rendered. In addition, they might have to pay a deductible if they choose to go outside the network, or pay the difference between what the in-network and out-of-network doctors charge.

Traditional Indemnity Plans, or Fee for Service

At one time, most people had traditional indemnity coverage, also known as a fee-for-service plan. FFS plans are sort of like auto insurance: you pay a certain amount of your medical expenses up front in the form of a deductible, and the insurance company pays the majority of the bill thereafter.

Traditionally, preventive-care services such as annual checkups are not covered under these plans. However, as evidence increases that preventive care can prevent more costly illnesses down the road, some FFS insurers are now including preventive care.

For many years, FFS coverage was the standard form of health insurance. You have freedom when it comes to choosing doctors, hospitals, and other health-care providers. You can refer yourself to any specialist without getting permission, and the insurance company does not get to decide whether the visit was necessary or not.

On the downside, FFS plans usually involve more out-of-pocket expenses. You usually must pay hundreds or even thousands of dollars in deductibles before the insurance company starts paying for medical services. Once you have paid the deductible, the insurer will contribute about 70–80 percent of any medical bills. You may have to pay up front and then submit the bill for reimbursement, or your provider may bill your insurer directly.

Under FFS plans, insurers will usually pay for only "reasonable and customary" (also known as Usual Customary Rates, or UCR) medical expenses, taking into account what other practitioners in the area charge for similar services. If your doctor happens to charge more than the amount the insurance company considers "reasonable and customary," you will probably have to make up the difference yourself. An FFS is the most expensive type of insurance plan in comparison to an HMO and a PPO, but for those who can afford them, an FFS offers the most freedom and flexibility.

HOW TO CHOOSE A MANAGED-CARE PLAN FOR YOUR COMPANY

Deciding on a group health insurance plan for your company is critical—especially when you consider that after paid vacation, health insurance is the most important benefit to employees.

Comparing Insurance Options

Before constructing or choosing a health plan, employers should find out what their employees want as well as what is currently covered in your geographic market. After discussing options and controlling their employees' expectations, small business owners should contact a licensed insurance broker, who should be able to provide a full explanation of the various choices available.

When reviewing your insurance options with a broker, ask the following questions:

> Is the insurance carrier licensed, accredited, reputable, and financially secure?
> How often are policies renewed—every six months or each year?
> Is the plan easy to administer or will it require a benefits administrator?
> Are claims processed and paid quickly?
> Does the insurer provide educational and other communications materials to employees and a website to access policy or coverage information?
> Does the insurer underwrite the policy as a group, as individuals, or both?
> Does the managed-care plan provide sufficient financial incentive to encourage employees to select network providers?

In addition to price quotes, it is a good idea to collect full proposals from insurers, including information about their customer services and claims-paying abilities.

When comparing health-care plans, you should keep certain things in mind. These include:

Affordability of Coverage

> How much will the plan cost the company on a monthly basis?
> Should you insure just for major medical expenses or for all medical expenses?
> Are there deductibles to pay before the insurance kicks in?
> After the deductible, what part of the cost is covered by the plan?
> How much more does it cost to see a provider outside the plan?

Scope of Coverage

- What doctors, hospitals, and other providers are part of the plan?
- Are there enough of the kinds of doctors you would expect to have?
- Are the providers located conveniently for your employees?
- Does the plan require permission for specialist referrals?
- Are there limits to how much the plan will cover?
- Does the plan cover the expenses of delivering a baby?
- Does the plan include prescription drugs?
- Does the plan include drug and alcohol treatment, mental health care, home health care, hospice care, physical therapy, and so-called experimental treatments?
- Is an Employee Assistance Program (EAP) available through the plan?

Quality of Coverage

- How do independent government organizations rate the plan?
- What do friends say about their experience with the plan?
- What does a doctor say about her experience with the plan?
- Can you provide a list of other local companies who use this plan as references?

OBTAINING HEALTH INSURANCE FOR YOUR EMPLOYEES

Depending on how many employees you have and what kind of coverage you would like to provide them, there are three different ways of obtaining health insurance for your employees:

- Through an insurance broker
- Through a professional association
- Directly from a health insurance company

EMPLOYER-SPONSORED RETIREMENT PLANS

A study by National Small Business United and Arthur Andersen revealed that only 28 percent of small and medium-size businesses offer retirement benefits to their full-time employees. Many small businesses just can't afford to sponsor retirement plans. For example, annual administrative costs for 401(k) plans can cost $5,000 or more per employee.

But a 401(k) plan is just one option. Before you dismiss the idea of sponsoring a retirement plan, consider all the choices—401(k), SIMPLE IRA, profit-sharing plan, money-purchase plan, SEP IRA, and Keogh plan—to determine whether you want to offer, or can afford to offer, one to your employees.

401(k)

A 401(k) is the most common type of company-sponsored savings plan. Any business with one or more employees can set one up. Employees can contribute up to $10,000 each year to their 401(k), and employers can choose if and how much they want to add. However, the combined contribution cannot exceed $30,000 or be more than 15 percent of the worker's yearly compensation.

A 401(k) allows employees to contribute more tax-deferred money toward their retirement than other savings options. However, 401(k) plans are costly. Establishing and administering a plan requires the involvement of a third-party administrator or financial institution, and yearly costs can exceed $5,000 per employee.

Simply put, a 401(k) plan is a tax-deferred investment and savings plan that acts as a personal pension fund for employees. It allows employees of corporations and private companies to save and invest for their own retirement, as opposed to grandfather's union pension fund of yore.

Under the typical 401(k) plan, employees can contribute up to 10 percent or more of their compensation on a before-tax basis, and their employer will match some of these contributions. Both the contributions and the investment earnings can grow tax-deferred until withdrawal, which is usually when the employee retires, at which time they are taxed as ordinary income.

So what choices do you, as a small business owner, have about what kind of 401(k) plan to establish? Here are a few of the main issues.

Employee and Employer Contributions. You can establish a plan that provides for only elective contributions from employees, or one where you match contributions. Matching employee contributions is the usual practice, and this option gives employees a much greater incentive to participate.

Be careful. This could become a cost that you can't control, since you can't determine how much an employee contributes. You can, however, set a percentage limit on your contributions; you'll match up to 3 percent, for instance. Sometimes high employee contribution rates create pressure on employers to provide salary increases to cover plan contributions, which should be a consideration.

Investment Practice. Funds in the account must be invested. Do you want your employees making their own investment plans, or choosing among a few specified alternatives? A wide field of investment choices is attractive, but it increases administration time and costs.

Borrowing. Because 401(k) plans usually charge penalties for early withdrawals, some plans allow employees to borrow against their money, with interest. While this increases the attraction of participation among lower-paid employees, it does increase the administrative costs.

Many small businesses simply prefer to work with an administrator, removing much of the hassle of taking care of the plan themselves. If you choose such an option, it's good to find a plan that provides a comprehensive, cost-effective package with sufficient flexibility to adapt to your growing company's future needs.

"Turnkey" packages that offer such services as advanced record keeping with daily valuation, trusteeship and reporting, employee communication materials, and plan investments are popular.

Try to find a packaged plan that offers a wider range of investment products for employees to choose from and comprehensive administrative support and record keeping.

SIMPLE IRA

A savings incentive match plan (SIMPLE) IRA is a tax-deferred retirement plan for sole proprietors or small businesses with fewer than 100 employees. Companies that do not maintain or contribute to other retirement plans can set up SIMPLE IRAs.

Under a SIMPLE IRA, employees can contribute up to $6,000 per year; employers must match the employee's contribution (up to 3 percent of the employee's yearly compensation) or contribute an amount equal to 2 percent of the employee's salary. With the exception of contribution limits, SIMPLE IRAs are subject to the same rules as standard IRAs.

Profit–Sharing Plan

Profit-sharing plans, which were initially developed to encourage hard work and loyalty, allow companies to set aside money for their employees during profitable years. The company invests the money, and employees pay taxes only when the money is distributed, generally when the employee retires.

Profit-sharing plans are a good option for small businesses because they offer the greatest flexibility; an employer can contribute to the plan in profitable years and not contribute in lean years. Profit-sharing plans are also relatively easy to administer.

Money–Purchase Plan

Money-purchase plans are similar to profit-sharing plans except that they obligate the employer to contribute a predetermined amount outlined in the terms of the plan. This means that a business must contribute even in years when it doesn't turn a profit. Employees may contribute up to 25 percent of their annual salary, or a maximum of $30,000 a year.

SEP IRA

Any business that doesn't already maintain another retirement plan can sponsor a simplified employee pension (SEP) IRA. The plan is funded by the employer and is easy to set up and maintain.

The maximum annual contribution for a SEP IRA is 15 percent of the employee's yearly compensation, or up to $24,000. Employers can decide each year whether or not to contribute funds to a SEP IRA.

Keogh Plan

A Keogh plan is a tax-deferred retirement savings plan for self-employed individuals. Although the exact contribution limits depend on the type of Keogh plan, in general, a self-employed individual may contribute a maximum of $30,000 to a Keogh plan and deduct that amount from his taxable income.

For more information about each type of retirement plan, visit the U.S. Pension and Welfare Benefit Administration's web site.

PAID TIME OFF (PTO) OR VACATION—WHICH IS RIGHT FOR YOU?

Paid Time Off, or PTO, is the most popular version of time off for employees in small, early-stage and progressive companies used today. PTO is a break from the traditional "Vacation Plan" of most employers in that it combines all three of the major time-off options offered (i.e. vacation, sick days, and personal time) and bundles them under one title and one accrual of time. For example, some employers might offer two (2) weeks of vacation time, five (5) sick days, and two (2) personal days a year usually then governed by three separate policies, guidelines, or rules for how and when they are to be used (for example, a sick day can only be a sick day if you have a doctor's excuse—which now forces the employee to use their medical benefits when maybe all they need is a day or two in bed to recover from the flu). PTO combines all three under one title and accounts for more days than a traditional vacation policy, say 17 days in this instance. But employees can take the days for any reason without having to make a designation of sick time, vacation, or personal. It rewards all employees. Traditionally, employers, more specifically managers, have frowned upon employees who used sick or personal time—even though it's an offered benefit—as if those individuals were taking advantage of the good will of the employer. Either it's a benefit or it isn't, and PTO eliminates the negative connotation managers might, could, or would use against employees for using a benefit they were offered as a condition of employment.

Question	Answer
1. What is paid time off (PTO)?	It is a fixed number of days for you to use for your personal life needs, i.e., your own illness, the illness of a family member, school events, vacation, and other personal needs. You decide how to use your allotted days so that you can balance your work and personal life needs. This is over and beyond designated and floating holidays.
2. Why did [YOUR COMPANY] select a PTO policy?	During a recent review, [YOUR COMPANY] determined that our current time away from work policy was not competitive with those offered by other companies in our sector. The analysis revealed a strong trend toward a PTO model. The new PTO policy will assist [YOUR COMPANY] in attracting and retaining employees.
3. Who is covered under the new PTO policy?	U.S. regular and extended temporary employees are covered by this new policy if they work 20 or more hours per week.
4. Why is PTO being implemented in some divisions and not in others?	[YOUR COMPANY] determined that each business group should decide whether or not the new PTO policy was appropriate to meet its business needs. In general, [YOUR COMPANY], in order to meet competitive needs, decided to move to the PTO model.
5. When can I use PTO?	You can use PTO for your own illness, the illness of a family member, school events, vacation, or other personal needs.
6. What does PTO not cover?	Bereavement, jury duty, military leave, designated holidays, and floating holidays are covered under separate policies.
7. Why are personal sick days included in PTO?	A PTO policy gives employees more discretion and flexibility in managing their time away from work. If necessary, you can use PTO when you are sick. In the event that you remain healthy, you are able to use PTO for vacation or other personal needs.
8. How is my new PTO accrual rate determined?	It is based on your anniversary date. For example, if your 5-year anniversary date is March 4, 20___ , then you begin accruing at the increased accrual rate (25 days) on that date.
9. What is the new PTO accrual schedule?	The following PTO schedule is effective March 1, 20__. Your PTO accrues daily and will be indicated on each payroll advice.

Regular and Extended Temporary Employees Working 30 or More Hours per Week

Years of Service	Days	12-Month Accrual	Accrual Maximum	Biweekly Accrual	Weekly Accrual
< 5 years	20	160 hours	320 hours	6.20 hours	3.10 hours
5, but < 15 years	25	200 hours	400 hours	7.70 hours	3.85 hours
15+ years	30	240 hours	480 hours	9.24 hours	4.62 hours

TABLE 9-1 (CONTINUED)

Question	Answer
10. What happens to my unused PTO at the end of a year?	You will be able to carry over unused PTO time up to a maximum of two times your 12-month accrual. For example, if your 12-month accrual is 20 days (160 hours), you continue to earn additional hours until your accrual reaches 40 days (320 hours).
11. Will my current accrued vacation/PTO be maintained under the new PTO policy?	Yes. Your accrued balance will be transferred and become part of your new PTO. You will start accruing PTO according to the new schedule. Therefore, if your annual accrual is 30 days (240 hours), you will be able to accrue up to 60 days (480 hours) before you reach the maximum accrual.
12. Can I use PTO time before it has been accrued?	No. In order to be paid for your time off, you should have PTO accrued.
13. What if I have used all of my PTO time and I am sick for 2 days?	You will not be paid for the 2 days.
14. What if I am sick or injured for more than 5 workdays?	If you are unable to work because of a qualified disability, you are eligible for short-term/salary continuation benefits after 5 workdays (7 calendar days). If you have accrued PTO, you will use it during this 5-day waiting period. However, in the event that you have exhausted your PTO, you will not be paid for this time.
15. Does the new PTO policy replace the Family and Medical Leave Act (FMLA)?	No. The Federal Family and Medical Leave Act provides you with up to 12 weeks of unpaid leave for certain qualifying reasons. Accrued PTO can be used to supplement unpaid FMLA time.
16. Can I take unpaid time without using my PTO days?	No. If you have PTO accrued, it must be used unless you have an approved personal or FMLA leave.
17. Will I receive additional vacation time if I use all of my PTO for sickness?	No. However, after you are out for 5 consecutive workdays because of an illness, you may qualify for short-term/salary continuation benefits. Keep in mind that if you have 20 PTO days, you would have to be sick for 5 days on at least four different occasions in order to exhaust your PTO.
18. Can I take time off under the new PTO policy without advance approval?	PTO time should be prearranged with your supervisor whenever possible. You are encouraged to plan your time off as far in advance as possible to enable your supervisor to plan for your absence.
19. Will new employees accrue PTO?	Yes. New employees are immediately eligible for PTO.
20. What happens to my PTO if I leave the company?	Your unused PTO will be paid to you upon your termination, unlike sick days, which are not paid unless they are taken.

VACATION POLICIES

Here is a sample vacation policy that most employers might use. It helps define how many days of vacation your employees will earn and when and how they can take them. It also describes at what intervals there will be increases in the amount of vacation time you will accrue, generally coinciding with years of service.

Example

At the end of the employee's first year as a full-time employee of [YOUR COMPANY], an employee is entitled to [number] days of paid vacation. The employee's vacation days increase to [number] days after 5 years of continuous employment with [YOUR COMPANY], [number] days after 15 years of continuous employment with [YOUR COMPANY], and [number] days after 30 years of continuous employment with [YOUR COMPANY].

Vacation time may be taken in increments of one day, but in all cases must be prescheduled and preapproved. One day of vacation for every five days that an employee is entitled to may be carried over to the following year, but must be used before [date].

[YOUR COMPANY] does not provide paid vacation time for part-time employees.

Vacation Pay

Vacation pay is the employee's regular rate of pay, excluding overtime or holiday premiums. If the employee's regular rate of pay varies from week to week, the employee's vacation pay will equal the employee's average weekly hours or scheduled hours in the previous calendar quarter, not to exceed 40 hours.

Pay will not be granted in lieu of vacation time not taken.

Scheduling Vacations

[YOUR COMPANY] will attempt to grant all employees vacation at the time they desire to take it. However, [YOUR COMPANY] must maintain adequate staffing at all times. Therefore, vacations must be scheduled in advance and with prior written approval.

Where conflicts develop, they will be resolved as fairly as possible. Preference will be given to the more senior employee, the employee who can demonstrate the greater need for vacation at the conflicting time, or the employee who makes the earliest request.

[The following plantwide shutdown clause may be removed if it does not apply to your circumstances.]

Plantwide Shutdown

It is [YOUR COMPANY] practice to have an annual shutdown of [period of time] during the month of [month]. All employees, with the exception of essential personnel, will take their normal vacations at this time. For those employees who are entitled to more than 10 days of vacation, the balance of that vacation must be scheduled. Employees who have been employed for less than one year receive paid vacation in the amount accrued as of the annual plant shutdown, provided that they have completed six months of service at [YOUR COMPANY].

Holiday or Illness During Vacation

When a holiday occurs during the employee's vacation time, the employee will still receive pay for the holiday in addition to the employee's vacation pay, or the employee may select another day off.

If the employee is hospitalized while on vacation, the time from the date of the employee's hospitalization until the employee's doctor releases the employee may, at the employee's option, be charged against the employee's short-term disability benefits, rather than against the employee's vacation time.

If this happens, the employee must notify [YOUR COMPANY]. If the employee becomes ill while on vacation, but the employee is not hospitalized, the employee's absence is charged against vacation time.

Termination and Vacation Pay

When employment ends for any reason, vacation time earned but not taken by the employee will be included in the employee's final paycheck. At the same time, vacation time taken in advance will be deducted from the final paycheck.

Vacation Accrual Methods

[The following is a sample vacation accrual chart. You can modify your vacation accruals to reflect additional credit for any factors that you feel deserve additional vacation as long as you are nondiscriminatory. If you make substantive changes to this policy, you should have your attorney look over the changes.]

Basic Seniority Accrual Method. Employees who have completed one year of service and who work a 5-day, 40-hour week are entitled to vacation as follows:

Service	Vacation entitlement in weeks/hours
After 1 year	1 week/40 hours
After 2 years	1 week plus 1 day/48 hours
After 3 years	1 week plus 2 days/56 hours
After 4 years	1 week plus 3 days/64 hours
After 5 years	2 weeks/80 hours
After 6 years	2 weeks/80 hours
After 7 years	2 weeks/80 hours
After 8 years	2 weeks plus 1 day/88 hours
After 9 years	2 weeks plus 2 days/96 hours
After 10 years	3 weeks/120 hours
After 11 years	3 weeks/120 hours
After 12 years	3 weeks/120 hours
After 13 years	3 weeks/120 hours
After 14 years	3 weeks/120 hours
After 15 years	3 weeks/120 hours
After 16 years	3 weeks plus 1 day/128 hours
After 17 years	3 weeks plus 1 day/128 hours
After 18 years	3 weeks plus 1 day/128 hours
After 19 years	3 weeks plus 2 days/136 hours
After 20 years	4 weeks/160 hours
After 21 years	4 weeks/160 hours
After 22 years	4 weeks/160 hours
After 23 years	4 weeks/160 hours
After 24 years	4 weeks/160 hours
After 25 years	5 weeks/200 hours

Vacation must be taken during the calendar year at times convenient to you and your supervisor.

Alternative Seniority Accrual Method. Vacation accrual is usually based on some element of seniority. Most companies reward long-term employees with additional vacation days. Illustrated here is another basic policy that accrues vacation based on years of service and is more generous than the first example.

Service	Vacation
6 months	1 week
1 year	2 weeks
2 years	2 weeks, 1 day
3 years	2 weeks, 2 days
4 years	2 weeks, 3 days
5 years	2 weeks, 4 days
6–10 years	3 weeks
11 years	3 weeks, 1 day
12 years	3 weeks, 2 days
13 years	3 weeks, 3 days
14 years	3 weeks, 4 days
15–24 years	4 weeks
25 or more years	5 weeks

Vacation Accrual for New Employees. Vacation accrual based on years of service does not address new employees who are hired after the beginning of the year. One way to provide vacation to new employees during the year of hire is to assign a schedule of vacation days based on the month of hire. The schedule could be set up as follows:

Month of Employment	Vacation Days
January	10 days
February	9 days
March	7 days

April	5 days
May	4 days
June	3 days
July	2 days
August	1 day
September–December	0 days

Simple Monthly Accrual. Another method of vacation accrual involves crediting employees with one day of vacation for each month of active employment. As employees gain seniority, they earn more days of vacation per month and are eligible to accrue a greater number of vacation days each year.

This type of accrual schedule might look like this:

1–5 years of service: an employee earns 1 day per month up to a maximum of 10 days per year.

6–15 years of service: an employee earns 1.5 days per month up to a maximum of 15 days per year.

16–25 years of service: an employee earns 2 days per month up to a maximum of 20 days per year.

26 or more years of service: an employee earns 2.5 days per month up to a maximum of 25 days per year.

Part-Time Accrual. Part-time employees may be eligible for vacation accrual on a pro rata basis based upon their regular workweek.

Thus, under the accrual schedule just given, a regular part-time employee in her first through fifth year of service who regularly works 20 hours per week could earn one vacation day per month up to a maximum of 10 days. One day of vacation would equal 4 hours (20 hours per week divided by 5 days in the week), and the maximum vacation time that could be earned would be 40 hours (10 days multiplied by 4 hours).

OTHER TIME OFF AND LEAVES

In addition to Paid Time Off and Vacations there are additional types of time off and leaves that employees may have under your company policies. This section attempts to capture all of those additional variations under one heading and to define them as described below. Not all employees may experience any or all of these in any given year, but employers provide this additional time in order that the employee might not have to sacrifice or lose precious PTO or vacation time.

SAMPLE POLICY

It is the intent of [YOUR COMPANY] to provide employees with vacation/paid time off. For the kind of leaves not falling under the definition of PTO, we have defined the following types of leave:

➤ Holidays
➤ Family and Medical Leave Act
➤ Short-term disability/salary continuation
➤ Workers' compensation
➤ Bereavement
➤ Jury duty
➤ Military leave
➤ Voting leave
➤ Non-FMLA leave
➤ Other time off without pay

Employees requesting other time off should fill out the Time Off Request Form.

Any request for a leave of absence must be made as far in advance as possible. Leaves will generally not be granted for more than a total of six months, although the leave period may be extended with the advance written approval of [YOUR COMPANY].

If local, state, or federal laws require a leave of absence under circumstances other than those described in this policy, then it is the policy of [YOUR COMPANY] to comply with applicable legal requirements.

Definitions

Holidays

Suggested Recognized Holidays

The following holidays are suggested to be recognized by [YOUR COMPANY] as paid holidays:

- New Year's Day
- Presidents' Day
- Memorial Day
- Independence Day
- Labor Day
- Thanksgiving Day
- Friday after Thanksgiving
- Christmas Day

Holiday Policies. An employee may take time off to observe religious holidays according to his or her religion. If available, a full day of unused (sick/personal) leave or a vacation day may be used for this purpose; otherwise, the time off is without pay.

We schedule all national holidays on the day designated by common business practice (generally observed by the U.S. banking industry).

If a holiday occurs during your scheduled vacation, you are permitted to take an extra day of vacation.

You are not eligible to receive holiday pay when you are on a leave of absence.

Family and Medical Leave Act. If you need extended time off for certain qualifying reasons, the federal Family and Medical Leave Act (FMLA) provides you with up to 12 weeks of unpaid leave. Vacation/paid time off does not replace FMLA. Vacation/paid time off can be used to supplement pay for this unpaid leave.

Short–Term Disability/Salary Continuation. If you are a regular or extended temporary employee working 30 or more hours per week, and you are unable to work because of a qualified disability, you may be eligible for short-term disability/salary continuation benefits after seven calendar days.

Workers' Compensation. If you are unable to work because of a qualified workers' compensation disability, you may use vacation/paid time off to cover the waiting period. However, if you later receive workers' compensation payment for this same period of time, your vacation/paid time off will not be adjusted.

Bereavement. [YOUR COMPANY] provides you with up to three days of paid bereavement leave for the death of an immediate family member, which includes a spouse, domestic partner, child (including stepchild), mother/mother-in-law, father/father-in-law, sister/sister-in-law, brother/brother-in-law, and grandparent/grandparent-in-law. In addition, [YOUR COMPANY] will provide one day of paid bereavement time in the event of the death of any family member or close friend.

Jury Duty. In the event that you are called to serve for short-term jury duty, you will be paid. You will be required to provide the proper documentation to your manager prior to serving. Long-term jury assignments may not be paid. Discuss the situation with your human resources representative to determine the status of your leave.

Military Leave. As a military reservist, if you are called for short-term military training, you will be paid your regular base pay less your military pay. You will be required to provide the proper documentation to your manager prior to the leave. If you are called to active full-time military duty, you will not be paid, and [YOUR COMPANY] will grant you an unpaid military leave of absence. Discuss the leave with your human resources representative.

Voting Leave. Employees who are eligible to vote in a regularly scheduled state primary or general election, an election to fill a vacancy in the U.S. Congress, an election to fill a vacancy in the state legislature, or a presidential primary may be absent from work for the purpose of voting during the morning of election day, without penalty or deduction from their pay. Employees who work an afternoon or evening shift are expected to take time outside of working hours to vote, if they wish to vote.

Non-FMLA Medical Leave. An unpaid medical leave of absence may be granted at the discretion of [YOUR COMPANY] to employees who are either ineligible for leave under the Family and Medical Leave Act or who have exhausted their entitlement to that leave.

A leave may be granted for 30 days and may be extended on a month-to-month basis for up to a maximum of six months, but will be reduced by the amount of any leave taken by the employee under any other [YOUR COMPANY] policy. Requests for extensions will be considered on a case-by-case basis.

A medical leave will not be granted unless the employee provides (1) a written request to [YOUR COMPANY]; (2) submission of medical documentation satisfactory to [YOUR COMPANY] that the employee has a serious health condition that precludes him or her from travel to and from work, being at work, or safely and satisfactorily performing the essential functions of his or her position with or without reasonable accommodation; and (3) approval by [YOUR COMPANY] (which is subject to its business needs).

If the employee does not return to work on the originally scheduled return date or request in advance an extension of the agreed-upon leave with appropriate and sufficient medical documentation, the employee will be deemed to have voluntarily terminated employment with [YOUR COMPANY].

Reinstatement from an extended leave of absence (beyond the initial 12 weeks of FMLA leave) is not guaranteed and will depend upon the availability of a vacancy for which the employee is qualified.

Also, after a medical leave of absence under the circumstances described here, the employee must be able to return to his or her original position if it is available or to a vacant position for which he or she is qualified. If the employee does not return to work after all authorized leave has been exhausted, employment will be terminated.

Reasonable Accommodation. If the employee is a person with a disability as defined in the Americans with Disabilities Act (ADA), [YOUR COMPANY] will also attempt to reasonably accommodate the employee's medical condition to enable him or her to perform the essential functions of his or her job.

Any accommodation must be medically necessary, effective, reasonable, and not an undue hardship upon [YOUR COMPANY] operations. If an employee cannot be accommodated to perform the duties of his or her original position, if available, we will attempt to place the employee in a vacant position for which he or she is qualified. Such a reassignment may be at the employee's current rate of pay or a lower rate of pay if an equivalent position for which the employee is qualified is not available.

The employee may meet with his or her supervisor to discuss possible means of accommodation. If [YOUR COMPANY] offers an effective, reasonable accommodation within the employee's medically necessary restrictions and the employee declines the accommodation, employment may be terminated and/or eligibility for short-term disability benefits may be lost, or such refusal may affect eligibility for workers' compensation benefits under applicable state law.

Medical Documentation. For purposes other than authorizing FMLA leave, [YOUR COMPANY] may request the employee to submit for review by its medical advisor complete copies of the relevant medical records pertaining to the medical condition for which the employee is requesting medical leave or reasonable accommodation. [YOUR COMPANY] also may request the employee to undergo a medical examination at [YOUR COMPANY]'s expense.

Failure to submit medical documentation or failure to undergo a requested medical examination may result in denial of the request for medical leave and/or reasonable accommodation.

All benefits shall be suspended during the medical leave. The employee will be notified of COBRA rights and will be required to pay the entire cost of the premium for health insurance, as well as the nominal administrative cost of maintaining the employee in the group plan.

Other Time Off Without Pay. A personal leave of absence may be granted for reasons other than the employee's own disability, family care, or military leave, depending on the employee's justification of need and on the effect that the absence will have on the department and/or [YOUR COMPANY].

A personal leave of absence is limited to 20 working days within a consecutive 24-month period unless an exception is preauthorized by the department vice president and the director of human resources. [YOUR COMPANY] reserves the right to refuse a personal leave request, regardless of reasons.

It is the intent of [YOUR COMPANY] to provide reemployment without loss of seniority for an employee who is on an approved personal leave of absence, but absolute guarantees are not possible. In some cases, a replacement may be hired.

Failure to return to work on the previously agreed-upon day will be regarded as voluntary termination. Mandatory usage of vacation/paid time off (if available) during this absence is required.

Please contact your human resources representative with questions.

PART 2

POSTEMPLOYMENT

CHAPTER 10

New-Employee Orientation (aka On-Boarding)

Do you remember being a new employee? Do you remember your mindset on the first day? It was probably a mix of anxiety, excitement, blissful ignorance, and irrational exuberance, right?

Now, do you remember what actually happened in your first week? In most cases, you were probably introduced to a few people, you signed a bunch of forms, and then you were set loose to do your destruction. Do you remember how quickly your enthusiasm and optimism waned?

What a missed opportunity for everyone. If you remember nothing else about new-employee orientation, carve this in stone:

"The primary purpose of orientation should be to *instill values*!"

Of course the employee needs to sign the required documents (W-4s, benefits enrollments, I-9s, and so on) and get a primer on key policies, but the experience of those first days can determine the success or failure of the employment relationship.

When I ask audiences, "How many of you have a new-employee orientation program?" some people raise their hands, and others don't. My response is, "Wrong!" You all have an orientation program. You just don't know it.

If you are not taking control of the first days of a new employee's experience, then someone else is, and it could be your worst employee! New employees have to learn the ropes somewhere, and if you aren't teaching them, then someone else is.

Someone may be telling them that certain reports are pure BS, so don't worry about spending a lot of time on them. Someone may be telling them which days you play golf in the morning, so don't worry about coming to work on time on Wednesdays. Get it?

Conversely, the best organizations to work for take new-employee orientation seriously. In fact, it is a well-orchestrated event. It's your meet and greet. It's your first (and lasting) impression!

There is no one right way to structure an orientation, but there are lots of wrong ways. Most important, however, is to create an outline that includes some values-instilling activities. Remember the "Why Work Here?" statement? This is where you prove it.

The first person to meet with the new employee should be his immediate supervisor or manager. This is the person who will be determining the new employee's quality of work life on a day-to-day basis. So think hard about what you say to the new hire during his orientation. The number one reason why people leave an organization is their day-to-day relationship with their immediate supervisor. That's what determines "Why Work Here?" on an individual basis.

For many people, on the first day, their self-confidence and enthusiasm about a new job give way to anxiety and confusion. (What am I doing here? What do they expect of me? Whom can I go to for help?) How long this mental mayhem lasts—an hour or a few months—can depend a great deal on employee orientation.

Orientation is, in fact, a training opportunity that promotes organizational effectiveness right from the start of a person's employment. Orientation speeds up the adaptation process; it helps the new employee feel comfortable at your organization. The more successful your orientation program, the sooner your new employee will feel comfortable, and the sooner she will become productive on the job.

An unsuccessful orientation program can mean more than slow adaptation for your new employee. It can mean no adaptation, no subsiding of first-day anxieties, no clearing up of confusion. The result? Loss of interest in pursuing a career at your organization, poor work, untapped potential, and, ultimately, an increase in your employee turnover.

See the enclosed CD for several examples of checklists and other tools for bringing new employees on board.

CONDITIONS NECESSARY FOR SUCCESS

Certain conditions are essential for an effective orientation program.

1. All employees, existing and new, must understand the importance of orientation. Employees from entry to senior level must be made aware of the tie between orientation practices and productivity, and they must take orientation seriously.
2. Your organization must be willing to invest the time, effort, and resources necessary to develop and maintain an effective orientation program.
3. The orientation program must be flexible enough to address the diverse needs of your new employees, including differences in employees' positions, work schedules, experience levels, ages, and backgrounds.
4. One person or group within your organization must be ultimately responsible for the program. Though developing and conducting an orientation program may call for participation by many employees, holding one person or one specific group responsible ensures the ongoing effectiveness of the program.
5. The person or group that is ultimately responsible for orientation must devote the necessary time and effort to training all the others who are involved in implementing your program.
6. The person or group that is ultimately responsible must ensure that the orientation program remains current. It must periodically assess the needs of the organization and how the orientation program is meeting those needs, periodically survey program participants for opinions about the

effectiveness of the program, and continually explore opportunities for program improvement.

SUGGESTED ITEMS TO COVER DURING ORIENTATION

- Show an upbeat video on the history, values, awards, and accolades of the organization.
- Give the employee an "out-of-the-box" employee handbook that instills values and makes a great first impression (see the sample in the next chapter).
- Give the employee an official employee handbook (see the sample in the next chapter; there is also a copy on the CD).
  This handbook should explain:
  - How and when performance appraisals are conducted
  - How often salary may be increased and how those increases are determined
  - The benefits the company offers
  - Policies and procedures
  - Work hours, overtime, comp days, sick leave, funeral leave, military leave, jury duty, maternity/paternity leave, leaves of absence, performance probation, discipline, security, and so on
- Safety procedures, equipment, and supplies.
  - Explain to your new employee all federal, state, and local safety requirements, and those of your insurance provider—then follow them. This also may/should be covered in the policies and procedures manual and by discussion.
- Cover the office procedures, equipment, and supplies.
  - Explain the procedures for such things as sending correspondence (mail, e-mail, and so on). Show your new employee how the telephone system works, how to use the copy machine, where supplies are kept, and other such things.

- Give the new employee a facility tour.
- Prepare a welcome reception with coworkers (get a cake or bring in lunch).
- Have a box of business cards already printed up before the new employee gets there. (Business cards for everyone! See Chapter 2, "Recruitment.)
- Advise the new employee of your bird-dog employee referral bonus program (also covered in Chapter 2).
- Assign the new employee a buddy or mentor that she can go to as needed. (Make sure it is someone positive.)
- Help your new employee understand the type of organization that he has joined, why it's been successful, what the plans for the future are, and how to contribute.
- Explain the nature of the business.
  - Discuss the profile of the customers or clients, the functions of the various departments, the services and products offered, competitive products and organizations, and other such information with your new employee.
- Explain the organizational structure.
  - Explain the departments and reporting relationships, including the names and positions of personnel who are key to the new employee's job (also include the names of all top management).
  - Provide an organization chart showing all departments and reporting relationships. Also give your new employee a chart showing the structure of her department.
  - Introduce your new employee to all department coworkers and key personnel from other departments, especially those with whom he will be interacting.
  - Review the new employee's job description/success profile and performance criteria. (Give the new employee a copy of both.) Discuss the work objectives and performance expectations. Explain the performance appraisal process. Clarify any confusion over functions and responsibilities. Tell your new employee how her job fits in with and affects others in your organization. Emphasize the importance of

this particular job, and describe how it contributes to your organization's success.

➤ Explain what your organization expects of its employees in terms of work performance, productivity, work habits and ethics, and the like. Also discuss what the employee can expect from the organization in terms of equitable treatment, professional development opportunities, career advancement opportunities, and financial rewards.

➤ Professional development expectations.

➤ Discuss with your new employee the expectations that your organization has concerning his skills development and the types of training required.

➤ Discuss the norms and rules of expected behavior for your organization and its employees, including culture, philosophies, beliefs, and the organization's values, as well as personal appearance and dress code expectations.

TOURING YOUR ORGANIZATION

No matter who is conducting your organization tour, certain specific elements should be covered. Following are tips for planning effective facility tours. Keep the individual needs of your new employee in mind.

➤ Plan the route ahead of time, and include stops at all work areas relating to the new employee's job. On every tour, be sure to point out fire extinguishers, fire escapes, and exit stairways, and discuss evacuation procedures.

➤ Include in your plan a list of staff members that your new employee should meet on the tour.

➤ Consider how much time the tour will take. Make sure that it will not run too long; if it does, your new employee may lose focus.

New Employee Orientation Checklist

Employee: _____   Date: _____

Department: _____   Position: _____

Responsible Party: _____

Instructions: Greet your new employee as soon as he or she reports to work, and begin the orientation process as soon as possible. Check each section below as you complete it. Record "N/A" in the blanks where the item does not apply.

You may add, delete, or change items by using the template on the enclosed CD.

Areas to Cover

_____ Organization history, philosophies, values, goals, and managerial style

_____ Nature of the business

_____ Organizational structure

_____ Organization policies and procedures

_____ Organization compensation practices and benefits

_____ Safety procedures, equipment, and supplies

_____ Office procedures, equipment, and supplies

_____ Specific job requirements and expectations

_____ General performance expectations

_____ Professional development expectations

_____ Behavioral expectations

Facility Tour

_____ Time clock/time cards/time sheets—how to clock in and out (if applicable)

_____ Mailbox—where the employee will receive written communications

_____ Medical/first aid—location and contents

_____ Safety rules, evacuation procedures, equipment and supplies

_____ Restrooms/break rooms/vending machines/cafeteria

_____ Employee parking—designated for employee use

_____ Restricted areas (tool room, parts area, cashier's area, etc.)

_____ Introductions to managers and coworkers

MAKE A NEW EMPLOYEE'S FIRST DAY GO SMOOTHLY

Many new employees arrive for their first day of work excited and eager to begin, but also concerned about the uncertainties they will face that day. It is up to their employer to plan to make a new employee's first day go smoothly.

Without planning, the first day could be a nightmare for both of you—60 percent of employees who quit do so within their first 10 days on the job.

To start a new employee's day off right, decide in advance what the first day will include—what the employee will do and whom to meet. Let all the people in your office who will interact with the new employee on that first day know exactly when and what they are expected to contribute.

Start the first day right by being on time to greet the new employee. Be in an upbeat mood. Reiterate how glad you are to have her on board.

Then, show the new employee her or his workspace and where personal items can be store safely. Introduce the new employee to co-workers who sit nearby.

Then take a tour of the office. Point out the restroom, common areas, and the supply room. If the new employee's first day of work turns out to be a hectic one for you, or if you are unexpectedly called out of town, arrange for a coworker to take your place to perform the necessary introductions and answer the new employee's questions.

Next, complete the following new employee tasks:

➢ Have the new employee fill out any necessary employment or tax forms.
➢ Give the new employee a packet of information that includes a job description, performance expectations, schedules, how to record work hours, how to operate equipment or computer programs, and benefit materials. Briefly explain what each item is or have your company's human resource representative review this material with the new employee.
➢ Arrange to take the new employee to lunch or have another worker do so.
➢ Outline what the employee can expect for the rest of the first week. Does your company have an orientation program? Will this person have to attend certain training sessions? Is there job-specific information, such as a star

client or new products, on which the employee will be expected to get up to speed quickly?

> Allow a new employee time to review the company's past work and talk with coworkers about ongoing accounts and projects.

A new employee's first day is a great time to establish a good working relationship. Throughout the day, check in to see if the new employee might have any questions, and make the person feel comfortable about stopping by your desk with questions.

Make the person feel excited about the job and the company. Most important, make it clear that you are glad that the new person is on board.

NEW EMPLOYEE PAPERWORK

When a new employee comes for his first day of work, make sure that you have all the necessary paperwork ready to be reviewed and signed.

This new employee paperwork can include:

> Signed offer letter. Keep the signed offer letter in the new employee's personnel folder to document the start date, pay, title, and other such information.

> Employee handbook. If you have an employee handbook, get a receipt stating that the employee has received and reviewed it.

> IRS W-4 form. Each employee must complete this form for the company to determine the appropriate level of tax withholding.

> I-9 form. The U.S. Immigration and Nationalization Service requires that you fill out an I-9 form for each employee. This form is intended to prevent aliens who are not properly documented from working in a place of business.

> Employee benefit enrollment paperwork. If your company provides employee benefit programs such as medical insurance or retirement plans, the employee should sign up and provide relevant information, such as identifying dependents and making required elections.

➤ Trade secret agreement. This is the agreement requiring the employee to keep company information confidential.

➤ Employee emergency contact form. The employee states whom he or she would like to have contacted in the event of an emergency.

➤ Direct deposit form. If your company provides direct deposit of paychecks, this form initiates the direct deposits.

New Hire Checklist

Name: _____ Hire Date: _____

Dept.: _____ Manager: _____

Once the signed offer letter is received:

_____ Send a welcome letter

_____ Add to phone list

Paperwork:

_____ Benefits new hire packet

_____ Company new hire packet

Communications:

_____ Office key

_____ Building access key

_____ How to order office supplies

_____ Office tour

_____ Phone list

_____ Add to organization chart

_____ Add to personnel sheet

_____ Add to headcount plan

_____ Add to share data

_____ Add to birthday list

_____ Confirm information on personnel sheet

_____ Send out e-mail introduction

Information that is needed on the first day:

_____ Offer letter

_____ Confidentiality agreement

_____ Nondisclosure agreement

_____ Résumé

_____ I-9 with ID

_____ W-4 (forward to Payroll)

Information that is needed by the end of the week:

_____ Insurance enrollment forms

_____ 401(k) forms

_____ Business card order form

_____ H.R. forms: In case of emergency, and so on

_____ Direct deposit form

Form completed by:

Signature _____   Date _____

CHAPTER 11

Employee Handbooks

TWO VERSIONS FOR TWO DIFFERENT PURPOSES

Why in the world would you want to have two different employee handbooks? Remember the primary purpose of new employee orientation and bringing on board? *To instill values!*

The standard employee handbook does not accomplish that goal. Most employee handbooks are boring, legalistic documents full of heretofores and hereinafters, full of don'ts and shoulds, with a form that is signed in duplicate to confirm that the new employee has actually read the handbook and understood it, and is then filed in his personnel folder. Now, isn't that a warm and fuzzy welcome?

Not in lieu of, but *in addition to* the "formal" handbook (a template for which is on the CD), we need to have a version that accomplishes our primary goal: *to instill values!*

Following is an example of just such a handbook, which you can use as a thought starter to develop your own great first impression. It comes from a cable and wire company called Anixter, and it is a booklet small enough to fit in a shirt, suit, or blouse pocket. When you read this handbook, ask yourself how you might have reacted if you had been given one of these on your first day of employment.

Orientation Handbook

Our Philosophy

1. People come first.
2. Our word is our bond—we are reliable.
3. We are Serious about Service.
4. We cannot afford the luxury of a lousy day's business.
5. We want to be the best.
6. We are realists, and we believe in candor.
7. We are accessible and easy to do business with.
8. We are aggressive—we are doers—we work hard.
9. We are often pleased but never satisfied.
10. We properly reward our people.

Our Specialty

We are serious about service!

To make a better-than-average profit, you've got to have a better-than-average business.

Since we don't have proprietary products, our service must be outstanding.

Service is a state of mind. To give exceptional service, our people must really care—and they must have the desire to do it right and do it now.

Service costs money. So, we expect to get paid very well for being sensational.

Our motto: *Service Is Our Technology*®!

Customers and Suppliers

Customers are not dependent on us. We're dependent on them.

They're not an interruption of our work. They're the purpose of it.

We're not doing them a favor by serving them. They're doing us a favor by giving us the opportunity.

Customers bring us their needs. It's our job to handle them profitably, for them and for ourselves.

Customers are our passport to success. Without them, we can't get there.

And at _____, we treat Suppliers as Customers.

(So, substitute the word "Suppliers" for "Customers" and reread the above.)

Truth

We tell the *truth* to each other and to our customers and suppliers.

The whole story, not just part of it.

We don't stretch it, bend it, or avoid it.

And, if someone raises hell when you tell the truth . . . let them.

Just say it like it is.

One little lie and you're a liar!

Express Yourself

Think! Think often, think hard, and then say what you think.

Feel! Have strong feelings, and then express them.

And don't get mad when others do.

Enthusiasm

Enthusiasm is the greatest business asset in the world. It beats money and power and influence.

Enthusiasm tramples over opposition, storms its objectives, and overwhelms all obstacles.

Enthusiasm is Faith in Action—faith to remove barriers and achieve the miraculous.

Enthusiasm is contagious, so carry it in your attitude and manner. It will increase productivity, and it will bring joy and satisfaction to our people.

Enthusiasm brings results.

Change

There is nothing so constant as change.

Everything must change to grow.

So we welcome change because—

Change = Growth = Opportunity

Stuffed Shirts and Big Shots

Don't call me Mr. or Ms. because—

Everyone's on a first-name basis at _____.

Everyone.

If somebody calls you Ms. or Mr. _____, tell them that your name is Matilda or Alfred.

Let's grow *big*—but stay small like a family.

Without stuffed shirts.

Managers

Managers are regular people who have experience and knowledge that you can use to help you do your job better.

They have friends and contacts, can usually sell pretty well, and are able to take on special
projects. This gives you additional hands and feet. And two heads are always better
than one.

_____ managers work for you (not the other way around).

So use them!

Our Contribution

Each one of us must pay for him- or herself each day.

This allows us to have exceptional men and women working for the organization.

Strive to promote sales, control costs, and increase productivity each day.

After all, _____ 's business is your business.

Hierarchy

Hierarchy turns an organization into a pyramid.

Pyramids don't move, they just slowly crumble.

Everyone should do what he or she does best.

Our organization deserves to have the best talent working on its biggest problems—or best
opportunities.

So we will continually reshuffle our people (and their titles) to suit the needs of the
organization . . .

. . . without a hierarchy getting in the way.

Job Descriptions

[A blank page follows, meaning that people do what it takes to get the job done! Obviously, the
firm has job descriptions, but again, this handbook is "tongue in cheek" for effect.]

Organization Charts

[Another blank page follows, meaning the same as the previous one: The firm doesn't let structure
and bureaucracy overshadow results.]

Phones

We make our own calls.

We answer our own phones.

We're never "in a meeting" or "busy."

And no one at ——— ever asks,

"Who's calling?" [The rationale for this is that when you ask, "Who's calling?" it implies
that you have to be important enough to get through.]

First Class

We entertain first-class, always.

To do this we must have *first-class profit*.

So, think *first-class*, be *first-class*, and let's make the necessary profit to keep this organization a *first-class* place to work.

Expenses

This organization is your business home.

Live in it according to your lifestyle.

Just pretend that the organization's money you are spending is your own. (It's your organization.) And write your expense account so that it won't embarrass you when it's posted on the bulletin board.

Hiring

We don't hire people.

We invite them to join our organization and help us make it better.

Firing

We don't fire people.

We ask them to leave the organization and help them go where they can be productive.

Promotions and Transfers

Three questions must be answered in this order:

1. Does the person want to do it?
2. Can the person do it?
3. Will the person do it?

Just one No . . . and it's "No!"

Cash Flow

More should come in each month than goes out.

Compensation

Pay the producers what they're worth.

Ask nonproducers to improve, coach them for success, then address alternatives if they don't produce.

Our Climate

We work for fun and money.*

We believe in an open book.

We put issues on the table, work them out, then get down to growing the business.

*Is there any other reason to work?

Managing

Lead!

. . . or follow

. . . or get out of the way.

People

"People" is the first word in our business philosophy . . . and the last.

Our business—any business—is People.

If we take care of Our People, they will take care of Our Business.

Well, what do you think? This "values-instilling version" of the employee handbook is printed in a little 3×5 booklet. You give it to the new employee on day one, ask her to read it, and then ask her to comment on it.

Now, let's talk about the official employee handbook. Most organizations ask new employees to read it and to sign a form stating that they received a copy, read it, and understand it. Do you believe they actually did that? Of course not! But they do as they are told, sign the form, and stick the handbook away somewhere for future reference.

Most employees pull out the official employee handbook on only two occasions: (1) when they are in trouble, or (2) when they want or need something. Otherwise it just collects dust somewhere.

However, you still must have one. So, what follows is a sample list of applicable laws and a complete table of contents for an official employee handbook.

(The complete "fill in the blanks" template can be found on the enclosed CD.)

Employee Handbook Template

Disclaimer (to the Reader of This Kit)

This document is meant to be a guideline for developing an employee handbook, not a substitute for legal advice. The suggestions for content are general, and the final product should be reviewed by legal counsel, as laws are constantly changing.

Note that some areas in the complete Employee Handbook Template on the CD are printed in *colored text and in italics*. These policies apply to businesses with specific numbers of employees. Refer to the list of laws to determine if they apply to your workplace. You may not want to include them and accept liability that you do not need to accept.

You should always make sure to get employees to sign a receipt of acknowledgment, which establishes the importance of the information and how it applies to employees. This receipt also states that the handbook is not a contract of employment.

Why Have Handbooks?

If you have 10 or more employees, you may want to have a handbook to pass on information such as the following to employees:

Your expectations of your employees and what they can expect from the organization.

Your customer service policies.

The workplace rules, so that corrective action is easier.

What makes your business a good place to work?

Handbooks can also provide evidence on the side of the business to defend against discrimination or unemployment claims.

Handbooks need to be clear and reasonable without excessive detail, so that all employees can understand them.

How to Use This Template

1. Review the document and delete those policies that do not apply to your business.
2. Add your organization's name in place of [your company].
3. Add specific information in areas that are in bold italic type, such as benefits, holidays, and so on.
4. Review the document again for grammar and spelling (spell-check and grammar-check can help).
5. Save and print the document.
6. It is highly recommended that you have a qualified attorney who is familiar with your state's labor laws review the document.

7. Communicate with your employees about the handbook, and get a signed acknowledgment from each of them.

8. File the acknowledgment in each employee's personnel file.

9. Plan to review the handbook on an annual basis and make appropriate changes.

Communicating About the Handbook

It is recommended that you meet with your employees and go over the handbook with them rather than just handing it to them. This way, you can make sure that they understand the policies and other information. You should let them know that the meeting is not intended to discuss changes in the document, but rather to allow them to ask questions so that they can understand the information.

TABLE OF CONTENTS

CHAPTER 12

Federal Labor Laws

EMPLOYMENT CLASSIFICATIONS

When you are hired, you are classified in two ways: as exempt or nonexempt, and as full time, part time, or temporary. The full-time, part-time, or temporary status determines what benefits, if any, you are entitled to. The exempt or nonexempt status determines whether you are entitled to overtime pay or not.

Nonexempt and Exempt Employees

All employees are classified as either exempt or nonexempt. By law, employees in certain types of jobs are entitled to overtime pay for hours worked in excess of 8 hours per day or 40 hours per workweek. These employees are referred to as *nonexempt* from these policies. This means that they are not exempt from (and therefore should receive) overtime pay.

Exempt employees are managers, executives, professional staff, technical staff, outside sales representatives, officers, directors, owners, and others whose duties and responsibilities allow them to be "exempt" from overtime pay as provided by the federal Fair Labor Standards Act (FLSA) and any applicable state laws. If you are an exempt employee, you will be advised that you are in this classification at the time you are hired, transferred, or promoted.

Unless otherwise specified, the benefits that the company offers apply only to full-time employees. All other policies apply to all employees, with the exception of certain wage, salary, and time-off limitations that apply only to nonexempt employees (see the preceding definition). If you are unsure of which job classification your position fits into, please ask your human resource representative.

Full-Time Employees

An employee who works at least a 40-hour workweek is considered to be a full-time employee. Full-time employees are entitled to all of the benefits that the company offers.

Part-Time Employees

An employee who works less than a regular 40-hour workweek is considered to be a part-time employee. Part-time employees are entitled to some of the benefits that the company offers. Only the benefits that specifically mention part-time employee eligibility are available to part-time employees.

Temporary Employees

A company may hire employees for specific periods of time or for the completion of a specific project. An employee hired under these circumstances will be considered to be a temporary employee. The job assignment, work schedule, and duration of the position will be determined on an individual basis.

Normally, a temporary position will not exceed six months in duration, unless specifically extended by a written agreement. Summer employees are considered to be temporary employees.

Temporary employee are not eligible for the benefits that the company provides, except as granted on occasion, or to the extent required by provisions of state and federal laws.

Please note that any employee who exceeds 1,000 hours worked in a calendar year is eligible for certain benefits as outlined by the Department of Labor, which may include pension or other retirement-oriented benefits. Please consult your employment law attorney for assistance as it applies to you in your particular state.

FEDERAL LABOR LAWS BY NUMBER OF EMPLOYEES

Note: This should not be considered legal advice and may not be a comprehensive list, as laws are constantly changing. Check with professional HR sources, state or federal agencies, or legal counsel to verify what laws affect your workplace.

1–14 Employees

- Title VII of the Civil Rights Act of 1964 and the Civil Rights Act of 1991 (for employment agencies and labor organizations). See the section on 15–19 employees for other employers.
- Consumer Credit Protection Act of 1968
- Employee Polygraph Protection Act of 1988
- Employee Retirement Income Security Act of 1974 (ERISA) (if the organization offers benefits)
- Equal Pay Act of 1963
- Fair Credit Reporting Act of 1970 (FCRA)
- Fair Labor Standards Act of 1938 (FLSA)
- Federal Insurance Contributions Act of 1935 (FICA) (social security)
- Health Insurance Portability and Accountability Act of 1996 (HIPAA) (if the organization offers benefits)
- Immigration Reform and Control Act of 1986 (IRCA)
- Labor-Management Relations Act of 1947 (Taft-Hartley)
- National Labor Relations Act of 1935 (NLRA)
- Occupational Safety and Health Act of 1970 (OSHA)
- Uniform Guidelines on Employee Selection Procedures (1978)
- Uniformed Services Employment and Re-employment Rights Act of 1994

With 11–14 Employees, Add

- Occupational Safety and Health Act of 1970 (maintain record of job-related injuries and illnesses)

With 15–19 Employees, Add

- Title VII of the Civil Rights Act of 1964 and the Civil Rights Act of 1991
- Title I of the Americans with Disabilities Act of 1990 (ADA)

With 20–49 Employees, Add

- Age Discrimination in Employment Act of 1967(ADEA)
- Consolidated Omnibus Budget Reconciliation Act of 1985 (COBRA)

With 50 or More Employees, Add

- Family and Medical Leave Act of 1993 (FMLA)
- EEO-1 Report filed annually with the Equal Employment Opportunity Commission (EEOC) if the organization is a federal contractor

With 100 or More Employees, Add

- Worker Adjustment and Retraining Notification Act of 1988 (WARN)
- EEO-1 Report filed annually with the EEOC even if the organization is not a federal contractor

Federal Contractors, Add

- Executive Orders 11246 (1965), 11375 (1967), and 11478 (1969)
- Vocational Rehabilitation Act of 1973
- Drug-Free Workplace Act of 1988
- Vietnam-Era Veterans' Readjustment Assistance Act of 1974
- Davis-Bacon Act of 1931
- Copeland Act of 1934
- Walsh-Healey Public Contracts Act of 1936
- McNamara-O'Hara Service Contract Act of 1965 (SCA)

An HR policies and procedures audit should be conducted to evaluate your organization's compliance with these laws. To expedite this process, you will need:

- Copies of any employee policies and procedures
- Copies of any handbooks

- ➢ Copies of any departmental practices
- ➢ Copies of any division practices
- ➢ Review of all state and federal postings
- ➢ Review of all employee files

MOST PERTINENT LAWS DEFINED

The following review of applicable laws (federal) must be conducted as well as those state and local laws that apply:

Employee Files

Review all employee files for compliance documents.

HIPAA requires that all employee medical records be kept separate from general employee data for employee privacy protection.

ERISA

Review 401(k) plan or pension documents.

The Employee Retirement Income Security Act of 1974 (ERISA) is a federal law that sets minimum standards for most voluntarily established pension and health plans in private industry to protect individuals in these plans.

ERISA requires plans to provide participants with information about plan features and funding; provides fiduciary responsibilities for those who manage and control plan assets; requires plans to establish a grievance and appeals process for participants getting benefits from their plans; and gives participants the right to sue for benefits and breaches of fiduciary duty.

Equal Pay Act

Review employee wages based on gender.

The EPA provides that the employer may not pay lower wages to employees of one gender than it pays to employees of the other gender within the same establishment for equal work at jobs that require equal skill, effort, and responsibility, and that are performed under similar working conditions.

Fair Labor Standards Act

Review payroll records for the past three years.

 Review all positions for exempt vs. nonexempt status. This will be determined after a review of the newly written success profiles (job descriptions).

 The FLSA establishes minimum wage, overtime pay, recordkeeping, and youth employment standards affecting employees in the private sector and in federal, state, and local governments. As of August 2010, covered nonexempt workers are entitled to a minimum wage of not less than $7.25 per hour, effective July 24, 2009 (check for current rate). Overtime pay at a rate not less than one and one-half times the regular rate is required after 40 hours work per workweek.

1099 Independent Contractor Review

Review independent contractor agreements for the past three years for IRS 1099 compliance.

 A 1099 contractor, or, more accurately, an independent contractor, is a legal and tax-related term used in the United States to refer to the type of worker that contracts his services out to a business or businesses. The "1099" refers to the Internal Revenue Service (IRS) form that an independent contractor receives stating his income from a given business in a given tax year.

 A 1099 contractor is not an employee of the business or businesses with which he works; instead, he is an independent contractor, or consultant, who is considered to be self-employed.

Immigration Reform and Control Act

Review employee files for I-9s and records used.

 The Immigration Reform and Control Act (Public Law 99-603) was passed in order to control and deter illegal immigration to the United States. Its major provisions stipulate the legalization of undocumented aliens who had been continuously unlawfully present since 1982, legalization of certain agricultural workers, sanctions for employers who knowingly hire undocumented workers, and increased enforcement at U.S. borders.

National Labor Relations Act

The National Labor Relations Act (Wagner Act) is a 1935 U.S. federal law that limits the means that employers in the private sector may use to react to workers that organize labor unions, engage in collective bargaining, and take part in strikes and other forms of concerted activity in support of their demands.

Occupational Safety and Health Act

Review Form 200.

According to OSHA, an effective workplace safety and health management system at a small business work site will enable the employer to:

- Recognize and remove hazards from the work site.
- Protect an employer's workers from injury or illness.
- Prevent loss of life at an employer's work site.
- Cultivate informed and alert employees who take responsibility for their own and their coworkers' safety and for workplace safety as a whole.
- Improve employee morale.

Americans with Disabilities Act

Review the records of any employees with a disability (illness or injury)

Title I of the Americans with Disabilities Act prohibits private employers, state and local governments, employment agencies, and labor unions from discriminating against qualified individuals with disabilities in job application procedures, hiring, firing, advancement, compensation, job training, and other terms, conditions, and privileges of employment. The ADA covers employers with 15 or more employees, including state and local governments.

Age Discrimination in Employment Act

Review workforce metrics and separation files for trends.

The Age Discrimination in Employment Act of 1967 (ADEA) protects certain applicants and employees 40 years of age and older from discrimination on the basis of age in hiring, promotion, discharge, compensation, or terms, conditions, or privileges of employment.

COBRA

Review files of any employees on or offered COBRA benefits and their administration.

COBRA provides certain former employees, retirees, spouses, former spouses, and dependent children the right to temporary continuation of health coverage at group rates. This coverage, however, is available only when coverage is lost as a result of certain specific events.

Typically, group health coverage for COBRA participants is more expensive than health coverage for active employees. Employers usually pay part of the premium for active employees, while COBRA participants generally pay the entire premium themselves. Still, it is usually less expensive than individual health coverage.

Family and Medical Leave Act

Review files of employees who have requested or have been granted FMLA status, time records, medical documentation, and so on.

Covered employers must grant an eligible employee up to 12 workweeks of unpaid leave during any 12-month period for one or more of the following reasons:

- For the birth and care of the newborn child of the employee
- For placement with the employee of a child for adoption or foster care
- To care for an immediate family member (spouse, child, or parent) with a serious health condition
- To take medical leave when the employee is unable to work because of a serious health condition

EEO-1

Review all EEO-1 filings completed over the past five years.

The Employer Information EEO-1 survey is conducted annually under the authority of Public Law 88-352, Title VII of the Civil Rights Act of 1964, as amended by the Equal Employment Opportunity Act of 1972. All employers with 15 or more employees are covered by Public Law 88-352 and are required to keep employment records as specified by EEOC regulations. Based on the number of employees and federal contract activities, certain large employers are required to file an EEO-1 report on an annual basis.

Vietnam-Era Veterans' Readjustment Assistance Act

Review the Vietnam Veterans Employee Questionnaire.

Worker Adjustment and Retraining Notification Act (WARN)

Review all reductions in force that have occurred in the past three years.

The WARN Act helps ensure that workers receive advance notice in cases of qualified plant closings and mass layoffs. The U.S. Department of Labor has issued guides to provide workers and employers with an overview of their rights and responsibilities under the provisions of the WARN Act.

Drug-Free Workplace Act

Review all drug screenings that have occurred over the past three years.

The Drug-Free Workplace Advisor assists users in building tailored drug-free workplace policies and provides guidance on how to develop comprehensive drug-free workplace programs. It also provides information about the coverage and requirements of the Drug-Free Workplace Act of 1988.

Davis-Bacon Act

Required if the company has federal contracts.

The Davis-Bacon Act of 1931 is a U.S. federal law that established the requirement that contractors pay prevailing wages on public works projects. All federal government construction contracts, and most contracts for federally assisted construction over $2,000, must include provisions for paying workers on-site no less than the locally prevailing wages and benefits paid on similar projects.

Copeland Act

Review employee wages.

The "anti-kickback" section of the Copeland Act precludes a contractor or sub-contractor from inducing an employee to give up any part of the compensation to which she is entitled under her contract of employment. The act also requires the contractor and subcontractor to submit a weekly statement of the wages paid to each employee performing covered work during the preceding payroll period.

Walsh–Healey Public Contracts Act

Review employee wages. Required if the company has federal contracts.

This Act requires contractors engaged in the manufacturing or furnishing of materials, supplies, articles, or equipment to the U.S. government or the District of Columbia to pay employees who produce, assemble, handle, or ship goods under contracts exceeding $10,000 the federal minimum wage for all hours worked and time and one-half their regular rate of pay for all hours worked over 40 in a workweek.

McNamara-O'Hara Service Contract Act

Review employee wages. Required if the company has federal contracts.

This act applies to every contract entered into by the United States or the District of Columbia, the principal purpose of which is to furnish services to the United States through the use of service employees. The SCA requires contractors and subcontractors performing services on covered federal or District of Columbia contracts in excess of $2,500 to pay service employees in various classes no less than the monetary wage rates and to furnish fringe benefits found prevailing in the locality, or the rates (including prospective increases) contained in a predecessor contractor's collective bargaining agreement. Safety and health standards also apply to such contracts.

CHAPTER 13

Performance Management

PERFORMANCE REVIEW AND DEVELOPMENT

So you've finally hired the right person for the job, and you've made a great first impression through orientation. Now, the key is to keep that person and keep him performing.

As you should know by now, the number one reason that people "check out" (and that can be either mentally or physically) is always the answer to the question, "What's it like to work here?" The answer to that question is manyfold, but it is primarily a function of the person's day-to-day relationship with her immediate boss.

Every manager must become an effective "human resource" manager. That doesn't mean that he has to be an expert on all the technicalities of HR (labor law, benefits plan design, compensation, and so on). It means that he needs to be effective at coaching, communicating, motivating, recognizing, and all the other "ings" to ensure that your people are motivated to stay and motivated to excel.

Whenever you are developing an employee's job skills and are ready to implement training, it is very important that you have clear objectives and be as well organized as possible. Jumping into training without thinking through what you are going to do may cause your explanations to be incomplete and confusing. You also run the risk of damaging the employee's self-confidence by leaving her poorly prepared to tackle the new task.

So, before you begin working with your new employee, make sure you consider the following questions. These should form the foundation of your training plan, helping you prevent confusion and misunderstanding during skill development sessions.

- What is the task you want your new employee to learn?
- Why is it important?
- What should your new employee be able to do when the training is completed?
- What are the steps needed to perform the task?
- From your experience, what potential pitfalls will you need to overcome in order for your new employee to achieve success in developing his skills?
- How will you overcome these pitfalls?

The performance review and development templates on the following pages (and on the accompanying CD) will help you and your employees track their performance and plan their developmental activities.

Please note that these templates are not intended to be used as is. If you have been following the plan of this kit, you should now have job descriptions/success profiles. Before you create performance management tools, be sure that there is consistency between the performance expectations that have been established in the job description/success profile and the performance criteria identified in the template you are using.

Performance Review and Development Template 1

Employee
Title
Department
Review Period
Job Responsibilities
Please briefly describe.

Accomplishments
Please list this individual's top three accomplishments this year.

1.

2.

3.

Strengths
Please list this individual's top three strengths, and after each, give a specific example of an instance in which this strength was exemplified.

1.

2.

3.

Opportunities for Improvement
Please list three areas in which this individual could improve and develop performance.

1.

2.

3.

Organization Values
Please review the organization values. Indicate how well this employee has been exhibiting the values and provide comments and/or examples.

Team Values:
- Respect one another and honor diversity.
- Be straightforward and direct when dealing with one another, our customers, and our vendors.
- Balance work and personal lives.

Comments/Examples:

Our Customers Are Our Partners:
- Create solutions that add value to their business.
- Deliver high-quality products by doing high-quality work.

Balanced Risk Taking:
- Taking informed risks, balanced by the values of the team.
- Being nimble and innovative, no matter how large we grow.

Results Orientation:
- Maximize sustainable profitability for shareholders.
- Honor commitments to each other and to our customers.

Goals/Objectives for the Coming Year

Overall Performance Rating

[ ] **Outstanding:** Performance consistently far exceeds job requirements.

[ ] **Exceeds Expectations:** Performance consistently meets and frequently exceeds job requirements.

[ ] **Successful:** Performance fully meets job requirements.

[ ] **Needs Improvement:** Performance meets some, but not all, job requirements.

[ ] **Unsatisfactory:** Performance is below job requirements.

Comments:

Employee Signature

Date

Note: This signature indicates only receipt of the review, not agreement with it.

Manager Signature

Date

Up-One-Level Signature

Date

Managers

➢   Please obtain the appropriate signatures.

➢   Give the signed form to Human Resources by September 13th.

➢   Copies will be provided to you by Human Resources for use in the review.

Performance Review and Development Template 2

APPRAISAL PERIOD: _____ to _____ DATE: _____

NAME: _____ DEPT: _____

TITLE: _____

HIRE DATE: _____ DATE STARTED IN POSITION: _____

INSTRUCTIONS

In completing this appraisal, the following sequence should be followed:

1. Review the attached job description. Notify Human Resources of any changes in/additions to the job description.

2. Complete pages 1 and 2 by circling the appropriate numerical value

3. To determine the overall performance ranking (simple average) on page 3, add the numerical values together and divide by 8. **Note:** If the employee has supervisory responsibilities, complete the supervisory section as well. The divisor will then be 11.

4. Obtain the signature of your manager (Secondary Reviewer).

5. Complete the Employee Action Record for salary change recommendations or job title changes, if appropriate.

6. Submit the Performance Review and the Employee Action Record to Human Resources for approval signatures.

7. Upon receipt of approval signatures, the appraisal will be returned for discussion with the employee. The current job description will also be included. Have the *employee sign and date* the job description.

8. Once you discuss the appraisal with the employee and obtain his or her signature, return the Performance Appraisal to Human Resources for permanent filing.

JOB KNOWLEDGE

Knowledge of products, policies, and procedures; *or* knowledge of techniques, skills, equipment, procedures, and materials.

_____ Expert in the job; has thorough grasp of all phases of job.	5
_____ Very well informed; seldom requires assistance or instruction.	4
_____ Satisfactory job knowledge; understands and performs most phases of the job well; occasionally requires assistance or instruction.	3
_____ Limited knowledge of the job; further training required; frequently requires assistance or instruction.	2
_____ Lacks knowledge to perform the job properly.	1

QUALITY OF WORK

Freedom from errors and mistakes. Accuracy, quality of work in general.

_____ Highest quality possible; final job virtually perfect.	5
_____ Quality above average with very few errors and mistakes.	4
_____ Quality very satisfactory; usually produces error-free work.	3
_____ Room for improvement; frequent errors; work requires checking and redoing.	2
_____ Excessive errors and mistakes; very poor quality.	1

QUANTITY OF WORK

Work output of the employee.

_____ High-volume producer; always does more than is expected or required.	5

_____ Produces more than most; above average.	4
_____ Handles a satisfactory volume of work; occasionally does more than is required.	3
_____ Barely acceptable; low output; below average.	2
_____ Extremely low output; not acceptable.	1

RELIABILITY

The extent to which the employee can be depended upon to be available for work, do it properly, and complete it on time. The degree to which the employee is reliable, trustworthy, and persistent.

_____ Highly persistent; always gets the job done on time.	5
_____ Very reliable, above average; usually persists in spite of difficulties.	4
_____ Usually gets the job done on time; works well under pressure.	4
_____ Sometimes unreliable; will avoid responsibility; satisfied to do the bare minimum.	2
_____ Usually unreliable; does not accept responsibility; gives up easily.	1

INITIATIVE AND CREATIVITY

The ability to plan work and to go ahead with a task without being told every detail, and the ability to make constructive suggestions.

_____ Displays unusual drive and perseverance; anticipates needed actions; frequently suggests better ways of doing things.	5
_____ A self-starter; proceeds on own with little or no direction; progressive; makes some suggestions for improvement.	4
_____ Very good performance; shows initiative in completing tasks.	3
_____ Does not proceed on own; waits for direction; routine worker.	2
_____ Lacks initiative; less than satisfactory performance.	1

JUDGMENT

The extent to which the employee makes decisions that are sound. Ability to base decisions on fact rather than emotion.

_____ Uses exceptionally good judgment when analyzing facts and solving problems.	5
_____ Above-average judgment; thinking is very mature and sound.	4
_____ Handles most situations very well and makes sound decisions under normal circumstances.	3
_____ Uses questionable judgment at times; room for improvement.	2
_____ Uses poor judgment when dealing with people and situations.	1

COOPERATION

Willingness to work harmoniously with others in getting a job done. Readiness to respond positively to instructions and procedures.

____ Extremely cooperative; stimulates teamwork and good attitude in others.	5
____ Goes out of the way to cooperate and get along.	4
____ Cooperative; gets along well with others.	3
____ Indifferent; makes little effort to cooperate or is disruptive to the overall group or department.	2
____ Negative and hard to get along with.	1

ATTENDANCE
Faithfulness in coming to work daily and conforming to scheduled work hours.

____ Always regular and prompt; *perfect attendance*; absent only in rare emergencies.	5
____ Very prompt and regular in attendance; above average; preplanned absences.	4
____ Usually present and on time; normally preplanned absences.	3
____ Lax in attendance and/or reporting on time; improvement needed to meet required standards.	2
____ Often absent without sufficient reason and/or frequently reports to work late or leaves early.	1

COMPLETE THIS SECTION FOR SUPERVISORY PERSONNEL ONLY

PLANNING AND ORGANIZING
The ability to analyze work, set goals, develop plans of action, utilize time. Consider amount of supervision required and extent to which you can trust employee to carry out assignments conscientiously.

____ Exceptionally good planning and organizing skills; conscientious.	5
____ Above-average planning and organizing; usually carries out assignments conscientiously.	4
____ Average planning and organizing; occasionally requires assistance.	3
____ Room for improvement; frequently requires assistance.	2
____ Unacceptable planning and organizing skills.	1

DIRECTING AND CONTROLLING
The ability to create a motivating climate, achieve teamwork, train and develop, measure work in progress, take corrective action.

____ Exceptional leader; others look up to this employee.	5
____ Above average; usually, but not always, motivational.	4
____ Average; sometimes needs to be reminded of leadership role.	3

_____ Needs to improve motivational and teamwork skills.   2

_____ Unacceptable directing and controlling skills.   1

DECISION MAKING

The ability to make decisions and the quality and timeliness of those decisions.

_____ Exceptional decision-making abilities; decisions are made in a timely manner.   5

_____ Above-average decision-making abilities; usually makes sound and
timely decisions.   4

_____ Average; sometimes requires assistance in making decisions.   3

_____ Needs to improve decision making and/or timeliness of decisions.   2

_____ Unacceptable decisions and/or timeliness.   1

PERFORMANCE LEVELS

DISTINGUISHED (5)

Truly outstanding performance that results in extraordinary and exceptional accomplishments with significant contributions to the objectives of the department, division, group, or organization.

COMMENDABLE (4)

Consistently generates results above those expected of the position. Contributes in a superior manner to innovations, both technical and functional.

FULLY SATISFACTORY (3)

Good performance, with incumbent fulfilling all position requirements and on occasion generating results above those expected of the position.

NEEDS IMPROVEMENT (2)

Performance leaves room for improvement. This performance level may be the result of a new or inexperienced incumbent on the job or an incumbent not responding favorably to instruction.

MARGINAL (1)

Lowest performance level, which is clearly less than acceptable, and which is obviously well below minimum position requirements. Situation requires immediate review and action. Possible separation or reassignment is in order without significant and immediate performance improvement.

MANAGERIAL COMMENTS

Noteworthy strong areas of present performance:

_____

_____

_____

Areas requiring improvement in job performance:

_____
_____
_____

What has the employee done to improve performance from the previous review?

_____
_____
_____

Developmental plans:

_____
_____
_____

To what extent have previous plans been carried out?

_____
_____
_____

Overall Performance Rating (cumulative): _____

Divided by 8 (or 11): _____

Circle one category below:

1	2	3	4	5
Marginal	Needs Improvement	Fully Satisfactory	Commendable	Distinguished

*Manager must submit to the Department Head and Human Resources, prior to the performance discussion with the employee, a detailed plan to address "marginal" or "needs improvement" performers.

EMPLOYEE COMMENTS:

_____
_____
_____

SIGNATURES: Signatures acknowledge that this form was discussed and reviewed.

Prepared by: Approved by:

_____   _____   _____
Employee   Supervisor   Next Mgmt. Level
Date: _____   Date: _____   Date: _____

EMPLOYEE PERCEPTION SURVEYS

Even if you do everything according to this kit, you cannot just sit back and let things ride. Employee relations is a moving target, and performance improvement is an on-going, continuous, never-ending process. Just ask the Japanese. They call it *kaizen*.

The easiest way to keep tabs on the pulse of your people is to just ask! So, why do so few organizations do this? First, because they don't know how; and second, because they are afraid of the answers they may get.

In the following pages (and on the enclosed CD), you will find a template for an employee perception survey that asks really good organizational development questions, but not ones that will open a Pandora's box or create strife.

Notice that we do not call this an employee *attitude* survey. It may sound as if we are just playing word games, but attitude is just a subset of perceptions. And as we all know, perceptions aren't necessarily the same as reality.

In most continuous improvement textbooks, there are usually four possible phases of development. (See the guide to phases of continuous improvement that follows.) The survey in this kit measures which phase your organization is in based on five dimensions of continuous improvement.

These dimensions of continuous improvement are:

- ➢ Process improvement
- ➢ Employee involvement
- ➢ Employee enthusiasm
- ➢ Improved capability
- ➢ Customer focus

Read the descriptions on the next two pages and guesstimate where your people might perceive you to be. Obviously, Phase 4 is where everyone wants to be.

Phases of Continuous Improvement: Where Are We?

Phase 1—Getting Started	Phase 2—Expanding
Process Improvement Only a few can explain what a process is. Few organization processes are charted or mapped. Problems are seen as being caused by people, equipment, or materials, not processes. Most people are not working toward achieving specific goals.	**Process Improvement** Some employees know how to read a flowchart or process map. Critical processes have been mapped, but not displayed. Problems may be discussed in terms of a process. Processes are changed or addressed only when there is a problem.
Employee Involvement Limited opportunities for involvement are available. Involvement efforts are generally viewed with suspicion. Involvement of employees is blocked by some in leadership. First improvement teams have been formed.	**Employee Involvement** Less than half of employees participate in any formal involvement effort. Involvement efforts are generally accepted. Involvement efforts are given passive support by some in leadership. Two or more improvement teams have been formed.
Employee Enthusiasm Employee satisfaction is seldom discussed by leadership. Turnover is accepted as part of the business. Employee satisfaction is not linked to organizational performance. Employees are considered to be just workers.	**Employee Enthusiasm** Employee satisfaction is acknowledged when it becomes an issue (e.g., low morale). Employees are encouraged to voice concerns. Employee satisfaction efforts take place, but not on a regular basis. Employee turnover is acknowledged only when it becomes a problem.
Improved Capability Employees have limited opportunities for training and development. Expertise is hired, but not developed. Individual functional expertise is valued (technicians). Employees must prove their competence quickly.	**Improved Capability** Training tends to focus on select employees or jobs. Beyond formal programs, leadership recognizes the value of all-employee information-sharing events. Training is presented mostly in good times. Coaching and development takes place when problems arise.
Customer Focus Customers are discussed in negative terms. No process is in place to measure or use existing customer feedback. Limited actions are taken to meet standards or expectations for customer care. Focus is on organization needs.	**Customer Focus** Customer satisfaction is talked about, but not always acted on. Some customer satisfaction measures are in place, but most are subjective. Customer satisfaction efforts are focused in key departments. External customers are the focus for everyone.

Phase 3—Adapting

Process Improvement
Some employees can map or chart a process.
Problems are seen as being caused by people, equipment, materials, or processes.
Most processes have been mapped and displayed.
Critical processes are being measured.

Employee Involvement
About half of employees participate in some form of involvement.
Employee involvement efforts are less formal and are not limited to improvement teams.
Leadership supports expansion of opportunities for employee involvement.
Some improvement teams are second or third generation.

Employee Enthusiasm
Leadership is willing to monitor and survey employee perceptions.
Employee enthusiasm is a frequent topic of leadership.
Some efforts are in place to meet the mutual needs of employees and your organization (e.g., scheduling).
Employees are considered to be valuable resources.

Improved Capability
Leadership generally recognizes the value of training.
Frequent or routine efforts to share information are in place.
Leadership has tolerance for loss of productivity during training.
Whole groups or functions are given training.

Customer Focus
Customer feedback is seriously considered in organizational changes.
Customer measurements are beginning to be taken seriously.
Recognition that customer satisfaction is not enough exists.
Two types of customers are recognized: internal and external.

Phase 4—Reaching Out

Process Improvement
Process maps are clearly visible within the organization.
Process maps are frequently discussed and revised.
Processes are improved, even when problems are not evident.
All key processes are being measured.

Employee Involvement
Most employees participate in some form of involvement.
Multiple opportunities exist for employee involvement beyond improvement teams.
Leadership is beginning to use employee involvement to address business issues (e.g., slip in volume).
Employee involvement is not seen as a program.

Employee Enthusiasm
Leadership regularly monitors employee enthusiasm.
Employee longevity is reinforced and recognized.
Employee enthusiasm is treated as vital to your organization's performance.
Employee enthusiasm is the goal, not satisfaction.

Improved Capability
Comprehensive training and development efforts are in place.
Expertise is seen as coming through the development of current employees.
A plan to develop current employees or functions is in place.
Coaching takes place on a daily basis.

Customer Focus
Customer feedback drives organizational change.
Customer standards and expectations are taken seriously and measured.
Reward and recognition systems support customer enthusiasm.
Customer and organization needs are openly discussed.

Employee Perception Survey

Company Name:

_____

Directions

This survey is designed to show where our organization stands in terms of your perception. Your response will be combined with other responses from our organization to create one report. The results will then be used to improve the effectiveness of our organization. Please take a few minutes to complete this survey. When you are finished, return the survey as directed. Please do not place your name on this survey. All responses are confidential.

The following questions relate to Process Improvement efforts in our organization. Please check the *one* response to each question that you believe best describes our organization.

1. In our organization, when an ongoing problem is noticed, someone:
   - ➤ Tries to fix the problem without getting ideas from others.
   - ➤ Tries to fix the problem by getting ideas from others.
   - ➤ Tries to determine how the problem should be solved and who should help solve it.
   - ➤ Asks if the process that is in place caused the problem.

2. In our organization, most people have a good understanding of:
   - ➤ Their job only.
   - ➤ Most jobs in their department.
   - ➤ How their job affects other departments.
   - ➤ How their job affects the organization.

3. In our organization, most people work toward achieving:
   - ➤ No specific goals.
   - ➤ Individual goals.
   - ➤ Department goals.
   - ➤ Organization goals.

4. In our organization, processes or procedures are:
   - ➤ Rarely changed.
   - ➤ Changed only when there is a problem.
   - ➤ Reviewed and changed occasionally.
   - ➤ Continuously reviewed and improved.

The following questions relate to Employee Involvement at our organization. Please check the *one* response to each question that you believe best describes our organization.

5. When problems occur at our organization, employees:
   - ➤ Blame others or other departments.
   - ➤ Solve only those problems that affect their job.

- ➤ Work with others in their department to solve problems.
- ➤ Work with members of other departments to solve organization problems.

6. Employees at our organization:
   - ➤ Avoid problem-solving efforts (such as quality improvement teams, task forces, etc.).
   - ➤ Get involved in problem-solving efforts when asked.
   - ➤ Volunteer ideas for improving the organization's operations.
   - ➤ Encourage others to get involved in problem-solving efforts.

7. Employees at our organization:
   - ➤ Resist or ignore changes that will improve organization operations.
   - ➤ Comply with the changes, expecting that they will go away.
   - ➤ Take responsibility for making ideas to improve operations work.
   - ➤ Teach and coach others to make improvements.

8. Opportunities to get involved in problem-solving efforts at our organization:
   - ➤ Do not exist.
   - ➤ Are limited to formal improvement teams.
   - ➤ Extend to less formal improvement efforts (beyond improvement teams).
   - ➤ Are a way of doing business.

The following questions relate to Employee Enthusiasm at our organization. Please check the *one* response to each question that you believe best describes our organization.

9. In our organization:
   - ➤ Employee satisfaction is not important.
   - ➤ Employee satisfaction is acknowledged when it becomes an issue.
   - ➤ Improving employee satisfaction is a specific goal of our organization.
   - ➤ The management team promotes an environment in which all employees feel appreciated.

10. In our organization:
    - ➤ There are no organization-sponsored events for employees (e.g., outings, meetings, or BBQs).
    - ➤ There are events only for certain employees.
    - ➤ There are events for all employees.
    - ➤ There are events for all employees, and we all look forward to attending them.

11. In our organization:
    - ➤ Employee turnover is accepted as part of the business.
    - ➤ Employee turnover is acknowledged when it becomes a problem.
    - ➤ We try to keep employee turnover at a minimum because it affects the organization's success.
    - ➤ Continuous efforts are made to discover the causes of employee turnover and find ways to reduce it.

12. In our organization, employees are considered to be:
    - ➤ Workers.

> People.
> Valuable resources.
> Business partners.

The following questions relate to Improved Capability at our organization. Again, please check the *one* response to each question that you believe best describes our organization.

13. In our organization:
    > Being knowledgeable or skilled is not appreciated.
    > Knowledgeable or skilled people are hired, but there is no ongoing development of people through training.
    > There is ongoing development of people through training.
    > Employees are encouraged to learn and improve in their jobs on a daily basis.

14. In our organization, policies and procedures are:
    > Ignored.
    > Enforced inconsistently.
    > Enforced consistently.
    > Reviewed and evaluated to ensure that they are effective and fair.

15. In our organization:
    > There are limited opportunities for training or development.
    > Training and development efforts focus on certain employees and jobs as required.
    > Training and development is provided beyond what is required.
    > Training and development plans are in place to develop all employees and functions.

16. In our organization, employees are:
    > Not encouraged to look for improvement ideas.
    > Encouraged to look within their department for improvement ideas.
    > Encouraged to look throughout the entire organization for improvement ideas.
    > Encouraged to look to other businesses/areas for ideas to improve our organization.

The following questions refer to Customer Focus at our organization. While some of the statements in the survey may not exactly describe our organization, please check the *one* response that you believe best describes our organization.

17. Customer satisfaction information (such as customer letters, industry stats, Customer Satisfaction Indexes, etc.) is:
    > Not shared with employees.
    > Shared with some employees when necessary.
    > Shared with all employees regularly.
    > Shared with all employees regularly and used to make daily decisions.

18. Employees, including management:
    - Speak negatively about customers where they can be overheard by other customers.
    - Speak negatively about customers where they cannot be overheard by other customers.
    - Speak positively about customers.
    - Encourage one another to speak positively about all customers.

19. When working with customers, employees:
    - Focus on the organization's needs, not the customer's needs.
    - Focus on one customer need without understanding the customer's entire situation.
    - Focus on all of the customer's needs by asking questions to understand the entire situation.
    - Go out of their way to meet all of the customer's needs and make him or her feel welcome and comfortable.

20. Employees who go out of their way to exceed customers' expectations are:
    - Treated no differently from those who do not.
    - Complimented privately by their manager.
    - Recognized by their manager to their coworkers.
    - Recognized by management to all employees.

The following questions relate to the Support level at our organization. Please check the *one* response that you believe best describes our organization.

21. In our organization, management:
    - Does not encourage employees to act on their own.
    - Gives employees very limited authority.
    - Sometimes trusts employees to operate independently.
    - Trusts employees to do the right thing.

22. In our organization, your supervisor:
    - Has not informed you of your job requirements.
    - Has made your job requirements somewhat clear.
    - Explains his or her expectations of you in your job.
    - Meets with you to discuss shared expectations of you in your job.

23. Problem-solving teams:
    - Are not provided with what they need for meetings (e.g., time, a place, supplies).
    - Are provided with what they need for meetings.
    - Are provided with what they need for meetings and asked what they need if they are to succeed.
    - Are provided with all of the resources they need, including management's genuine interest and support.

24. Problem-solving teams:
    - Are not recognized for their achievements.

> Are privately complimented by management.
> Receive public recognition from management.
> Are recognized by all employees for their achievements.

25. I am, or have been, a member of a quality improvement or problem-solving team.
    ☐ Yes   ☐ No

26. I am a member of management.
    ☐ Yes   ☐ No

27. Please provide the following optional information.
    Please check the department in which you work. (Check one)
    > Sales & Marketing
    > Operations

    (Add or edit as appropriate for your organization.)
    > Other (Please specify) _____

Employee Survey Instructions

Employee Survey Purpose

1. To provide a simple model that the leadership team can use to determine the organization's progress in becoming an organization that incorporates continuous improvement.
2. To help increase employee awareness of continuous improvement and provide a means for involving all employees in the improvement process.
3. To provide managers with the feedback necessary for becoming more effective individual managers.

Administration Guidelines

1. Work with your management/leadership team to choose a date (a week or so in advance) for administering the survey. Try to choose a date when the least number of employees will be absent for business reasons, vacations, or holidays.
2. Communicate to everyone in your organization, either in person or by memo, the purpose and date of the survey. Clearly indicate that it is both

voluntary and strictly confidential. Note: It may be easier for some employees to complete the survey immediately before or after their normal work hours. If that is necessary, it should be compensated time.

3. Provide a designated place where employees can sit down at a table and complete the survey, e.g., a lunch area, conference room, or vacant office.

4. Monitor the survey location to ensure that employees have privacy while they are completing the survey.

5. Ask managers to plan for and allow employees to be gone from their work areas for a maximum of 30 minutes. Remind managers to be sure to have someone cover for their employees.

6. Provide pencils/pens, copies of blank surveys, and a box (similar to a ballot box) where employees can place their completed survey.

7. Encourage everyone in your organization to complete a survey.

Analyzing and Sharing Survey Results

1. If you use the Employee Perception Survey Results Calculator on the enclosed CD, the front worksheet is fed off the other two. Those next two worksheets are to separate managers from non-managers. Each survey participant has a set of rows, and the columns are the question number. Just put a 1 in each cell that the participant answered, and they are automatically added up and fed to the front worksheet.

2. Analysis of your survey results will assist your management team in identifying areas that:

    a. Employees and managers recognize as strengths.

    b. Employees and managers see as lagging in developing process improvements.

    c. Employees perceive as impeding progress to create action plans for improvement. Your leadership team may choose to invite employees to join a continuous improvement team to work on these areas.

3. The management team should develop a plan for sharing the results of this survey with all employees in your organization.

Employee Perception Survey Results—Sample

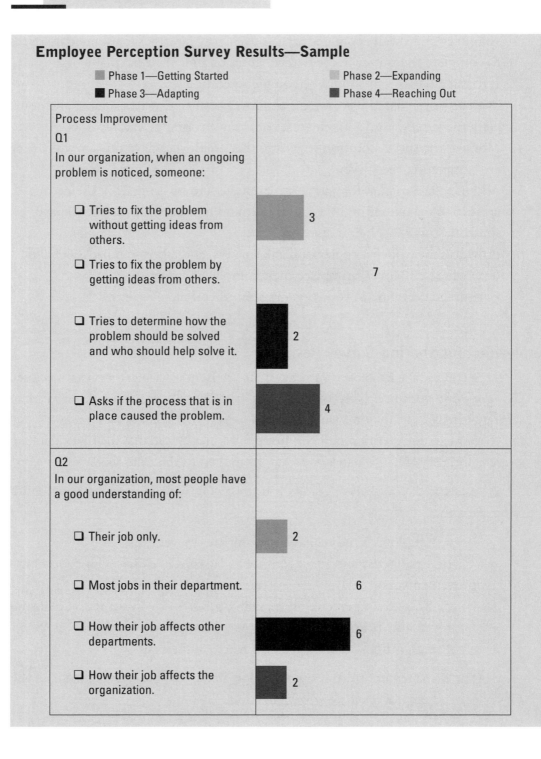

■ Phase 1—Getting Started   ■ Phase 2—Expanding
■ Phase 3—Adapting   ■ Phase 4—Reaching Out

Process Improvement

Q1

In our organization, when an ongoing problem is noticed, someone:

❑ Tries to fix the problem without getting ideas from others.   3

❑ Tries to fix the problem by getting ideas from others.   7

❑ Tries to determine how the problem should be solved and who should help solve it.   2

❑ Asks if the process that is in place caused the problem.   4

Q2

In our organization, most people have a good understanding of:

❑ Their job only.   2

❑ Most jobs in their department.   6

❑ How their job affects other departments.   6

❑ How their job affects the organization.   2

a. It is not necessary, nor is it appropriate, to share all of the details. However, a summary of the results should be shared.

b. This can be done in department meetings or in an all-employee meeting. It is not recommended that the results be communicated by memo or in some other written form without a meeting. You want to be able to orchestrate the discussion and interpretation, not leave it to others to figure out on their own.

c. Present the highlights, including those areas where there is a general consensus on your strengths and your opportunities for improvement, and where there are gaps in perception between departments or between management and non-management. Looking at the sample report given here, you could also present the bars in two colors, to show how many responses were from management and how many were from non-management.

EMPLOYEE RETENTION TOOLKIT

Why do employers concern themselves with the retention and turnover of their employees? Because it costs lots of money! Some sources believe that it can cost as much as two to three times the individual's annual salary to lose a good employee. Think about it. Not only do you lose the productivity of such employees while they are disgruntled and looking for another job, (in effect, they've checked out and are working on finding the new job, not working on the job you are paying them to do), you also have the following costs: the cost of recruitment (e.g., advertisements, time for candidate review, initial screenings, etc.); actual face-to-face interviewing and the lost time of everyone involved with the interview instead of working on their normal job responsibilities. Let's roll in the amount of time it takes a new employee to get up to speed, as well as that of the individuals who are responsible for getting them there. Some estimate that it can take anywhere from two to six months for new employees to be fully functional in a new job. So employers only get about 10 percent of that individual's productivity the first month and gradually work up to 90 percent+ by the sixth month.

What about missed opportunity? Think about the cost of losing potential customers who were about to close but turned away in the eleventh hour because they were buying the salesperson more than the product or service, or the mechanic you trusted and who always took care of you, but went somewhere else; or the hairdresser, manicurist; accountant; lawyer . . . You get the picture. Think about it on the personal front; do you buy from the salesperson who is a jerk or the person with whom you've developed some rapport? It's obvious. There is a lot of money invested in this process, as you can see. So it is critically important that employers develop a retention philosophy to retain the talent that they spent so much time bringing to their place of employment. Following are some tools that will help you think about innovative ways to do exactly that.

EMPLOYEE RETENTION TOOLKIT

Employee Relations Tools	Description
"Cease and desist" letters.	Drafted by attorney from top manager to counterpart.
Non-competes and intellectual property agreements.	Verify that these are legally defensible; variables include scope of job in industry, number of years, and geographic radius.
Focus groups.	Gather 8 to 12 employees with a neutral facilitator; maintain individual confidentiality; follow up on discussion items to preserve credibility.
Exit interviews conducted by department manager and HR.	Summarize and quantify results over time; spot trends; issue recommendations.

Compensation Tools	Description
Frequency and amount of salary increases.	Provide an accelerated schedule or amount for vulnerable groups, such as information systems professionals and engineers. Watch for morale issues in groups that do not receive equal treatment. Establish target percentile for pay structures in the marketplace.
Adjustments to salary structure.	Base these on marketplace movement, competition, workforce supply, and economic factors in the recruiting area. Adjust minimum, midpoint, and maximum amounts. Adjust the percentage of pay increases for various performance levels, depending on desired results.

Designate a percentage of compensation as "at risk."	Possible for both exempt and non-exempt employees. Base this on attaining preestablished business goals and meeting personal objectives.
Lump-sum payout.	Use if the employee is at or near the end of the salary grade. The employee receives a one-time payout for the entire year. This results in slower movement within the grade and allows time for the salary structure to advance based on changes in the marketplace. The company saves money, as the amount is not added to the base.
Retention bonuses and contracts.	The company provides lump-sum or annual cash payments or noncash perks. In return, the employee promises to remain at the company for the contracted period of time. Misconduct, poor performance, or litigation nullifies the contract.
Sign-on bonuses.	Granted upon hire. These provide extra compensation without affecting the salary structure.
Relocation payback agreements.	The employee agrees to pay back relocation benefits received if he or she leaves the company voluntarily before a contracted period of time. The employee signs the agreement prior to receiving benefits.
Technical training payback agreements.	The employee agrees to pay back training tuition funded by the company if he or she leaves voluntarily before a contracted period of time. The employee signs the agreement prior to receiving training.
Spot cash awards.	To award a special accomplishment or project work. There should be no stipulation of if or when the company will provide these on a continual basis. The surprise element has great impact.
Career counseling and outplacement packages.	Funding on packages can vary by level of position. Consistency is important. Employees can choose between the package of services and the cash value.

Benefits Tools	**Description**
Alter waiting period to qualify for benefits.	Shorten or eliminate the waiting period on group health coverage.
Base amount of company-paid premiums on tenure.	Prorate contribution levels based on service. After a given number of years, company pays entire premium. Other options are lower deductibles, higher copays,

preventive services, and spending accounts for health-care and child-care expenses.

Tuition reimbursements.	Increase the percentage of reimbursement or the range of courses covered. Reimburse for books and fees. Offer on-site courses on your premises given by a local college.
Introduce new programs.	Stock purchase plans, stock options, long-term care insurance, legal insurance, financial planning, benefits for same-sex partners, life insurance benefits for the terminally ill. Unusual plans are no longer restricted to non-exempts. The company pays all or part of the cost.
Subsidized child care.	Possible options include referrals, contractors, on-site, or discounts for off-site. Research any liability issues.
Employee services: on-premises dry cleaning, banking, grocery shopping, takeout catering.	Watch for heavy administration, company liability, legal exposure for companies with nonsolicitation rules.
"Total compensation" statements.	Issued to each employee annually; states the value of all compensation and benefit plans, company-paid taxes, vacation, and so on —"hidden paycheck" theme.

Scheduling Tools	Description
Sabbaticals.	Paid or unpaid. Can be earned after attainment of a given service level. Encourage research projects, grants, pursuing areas of special interest. Return to same or different position in the company. Prevent burnout.
Paid internships.	Offer to college juniors and above during summers. Make job offer prior to graduation.
Flexible scheduling arrangements.	Core hours when everyone must be at work; floating hours at either end. Good communications and team-work in the work group is a must.
Job shares.	Split workday, shift, workweek. Sometimes a transitional day is scheduled where both parties work the same day. Clear expectations and good communication between individuals are a must.
Rotational assignments.	Can be used for initial training or to enrich existing assignments. Assign specific tasks; develop checkpoints and deliverables to ensure a meaningful experience.

On-call arrangements.

Existing staff members pinch-hit for unexpected absences. "Virtual arrangements." Vary pay rates for being on call and for reporting.

Virtual office/telecommuting.

Saves office space and provides increased flexibility for employees. Liability and equipment issues. Hard to control productivity. Requires a skillful manager to be successful.

Workplace Enhancement Tools	**Description**
Relaxed dress code.	On selected days or every day. This can be used as a team award or incentive. Be sure to define expectations.
Separate locations for technical groups.	Off-site, think-tank environment. This liberates "techies" from the traditional corporate world.
Redeployment versus terminations.	Retrain to learn new skills. If possible, structure the job around the skills of the displaced worker. Use attrition and volunteers for transition packages to prevent terminations. Strategic decisions are needed about whom you want to have exit and when.
Meaningful new-hire orientations.	Infuse the culture of the organization. Communicate values; create a road map for success.
Timely performance appraisals.	A basic that is often overlooked. Tie managers' raises to meaningful, timely appraisals.
Effective dispute resolution procedures.	Peer review councils or a fair hearing process restore a feeling of control to employees and reduce third-party claims and legal expense.
Effective career paths.	Review career options regularly. Provide the tools needed to get there. Strengthen management development program and commitment to training; create career ladders within job families. Make employees accountable for their own future.

CHAPTER 14

Discipline, Termination, Reductions in Force, and Exit Procedures

Everything in this kit has been developed with the intention of reducing turnover and increasing productivity and morale. However, even in the best of organizations with the best of processes, there will be occasions when an employee isn't making the grade or the marriage just doesn't work. That's just reality.

In order to continue with the philosophy that employment is PR, how you discipline and terminate employees (if necessary) is just as critical as how you brought them on board. After all, they will still be in the community talking about you, good or bad.

So, let's start with attempting to save the employee. The purpose of progressive discipline is not to prepare a case for termination. It should be viewed as a bona fide effort to turn the employee's performance or behavior around. After all, we already have a significant investment in him, so our first objective should be to get a return on that investment.

Believe it or not, our underlying intentions can contribute to the outcome. If our goal is to save the person, we will approach the process with that expectation.

If our goal is just to set him up for a legal termination, then our mindset will be very different and nonconstructive.

PROGRESSIVE DISCIPLINE

Employers are often frustrated by the idea of a never-ending employment relationship with troublesome employees. They are dismayed when they are faced with the challenge of addressing performance or behavioral issues with employees who feel empowered by protection under one employment law or another.

Even nonunion employees are acutely aware of their rights, leaving employers feeling paralyzed and ill-equipped to act. However, employers can negotiate the confusing, intimidating path of discipline effectively and secure a successful outcome by maintaining two fundamental principles: (1) Employees deserve the opportunity to understand what is expected of them in terms of both performance and behavior, and (2) a warning notice is a tool that is used to explain to employees what is unacceptable and to give them the opportunity to change their behavior or performance through corrective action.

It is beneficial for employers to establish a written policy based on operating practicalities that clearly delineates who in the organization has the authority to administer discipline. For example, employers may wish to allow first-line supervisors to issue written warnings or suspensions, but to defer terminations to the human resource professionals in the organization.

The organization's policies and procedures should remain flexible enough to allow for necessary deviations. For example, policies should indicate the steps that can and may be taken, but will not necessarily be taken, to avoid the policy being construed as a binding agreement or unnecessarily tying the employer's hands.

Disciplinary action may take the form of verbal counseling, a written warning, a suspension without pay for a designated period of time, or dismissal. Generally speaking, discipline should be *progressive*, although there are circumstances in which some steps in the disciplinary process should be bypassed. It is a good idea to follow this policy regardless of the union status of employees and, in particular, to administer the practice consistently with respect to union and nonunion employees in organizations in which both exist.

Before disciplinary action is taken, the supervisor should review the employee's disciplinary record. Ideally, the supervisor should not terminate employees before consulting with a representative from human resources. Even in circumstances in which the likely outcome will be the employee's termination, the employee can be suspended pending investigation, and if the employee is ultimately terminated, that termination should be done in the proper, controlled environment in a professional manner.

What Is Progressive Discipline?

For discipline to be progressive, each related event or incident must trigger a response that is more severe. Each step in the process more strongly encourages the employee to modify his or her behavior. Generally speaking, unless a particular incident rises to the level of just cause for termination, many arbitrators have ruled that the requirement of progressive discipline has not been satisfied unless a suspension was administered prior to termination.

Some employers have adopted a two-track system for progressive discipline. In this system, discipline for attendance and/or tardiness involves progressive written warnings but *not* suspensions (the rationale being that a suspension rewards the employee with additional time off), while discipline for other performance or behavior issues includes suspending the employee. Employers with union workers should review collective bargaining agreements for language that covers the topic of progressive discipline.

The following is an example of a progressive disciplinary process:

Step 1: Verbal counseling. Place documentation of counseling in the employee's file, including the reason for counseling, the date and time of counseling, and who was present.

Step 2: First written warning.

Step 3: Second written warning, accompanied by a short suspension (usually one to three days).

Step 4: Third written warning with a long suspension (usually at least one work-week). This may also be the *final warning*.

Step 5: Termination.

Some serious infractions warrant skipping one or more steps and jumping to a higher level of discipline (very serious infractions such as fighting or theft may warrant termination as the first and only step). For very serious infractions, it may be appropriate to suspend an employee and contact the human resource department or legal counsel to review the incident.

For example, it may be advisable to suspend employees who were involved in a physical altercation because the organization's primary objective may be to remove the danger rather than to announce a termination and risk the escalation of a situation.

Warning Notices

Written warning notices, which are necessary for the documentation of disciplinary action, should follow the following guidelines:

1. They should be written on official forms. Do not use e-mail.
2. The specific date, time, and location of the infraction and the specific nature of the infraction should be detailed in the notice.
3. Avoid combining different infractions in a single warning notice (unless they are related, such as patterns of absence or lateness).
4. Check the employee's history. Warning notices should be sequential (check to see if the employee has already received a written warning for this type of offense). The notice should include the step of the discipline process (i.e., first written warning, second written warning, and so on).
5. Any suspension should be indicated specifically on the notice, including the number of days suspended and the dates.

6. The notice should state the next step that the employee should anticipate if the infraction is repeated (e.g., another occurrence of no-call/no-show will result in a one-week suspension).

7. The employee should be asked to sign the notice. If the employee refuses to sign, write that the employee refused to sign in the space and have a witness initial that the employee received a copy of the notice.

Warning notices are documents that the employer may need at unemployment hearings, at arbitrations, or in defense of wrongful termination or discrimination claims. Employees and union delegates should *not* write anything other than a signature on the notice. If the employee or delegate wishes to submit a written response, it should be on a separate sheet of paper and attached to the warning notice.

The interval between warning notices is very important. Warning notices issued one year or more before a second warning notice should be given little weight, unless both infractions are of a major or severe nature.

A Word About Verbal Counseling and Final Warnings

There's an old saying in labor relations: If it isn't in writing, it didn't happen. Even verbal counseling should be documented. The documentation, which should include the date and time of the session, serves to memorialize the session so that it can be referred to subsequently. The employee should be told that this is only a verbal counseling but should be asked to sign the documentation.

Generally speaking, an employee should be counseled only once. Sitting down and talking to an employee about an issue over and over usually just intimidates the employee, frustrates the supervisor, and negates the legitimacy of the progressive disciplinary process, not to mention that it undermines the manager's authority.

Similarly, when they deliver a *final warning* to an employee, managers should be prepared to stick to it. Attorneys representing employees *love* to see multiple final warnings; the more there are, the less they mean! The manager and the employee should both be aware that a final warning is just that—final. The only appropriate next step is termination. There is no going back.

Suspension

The rule of thumb is: the more serious the infraction, the longer the suspension. Suspensions should be for whole shifts. Having said that, sometimes it is necessary to send an employee home immediately, in the middle of a shift.

Many times, suspensions are given pending investigation. This is a dangerous necessity. When an employee is suspended pending investigation, it is imperative that the investigation be initiated immediately and that a concerted effort be made to conclude the investigation as quickly as possible.

Remember, if the investigation takes two weeks, the employee is suspended for those two weeks. After all is said and done, the infraction may not have warranted a two-week suspension, in which case the employee may be entitled to be paid for time not worked.

Occasionally, exempt employees must be suspended. An exempt employee, one who is exempt from the overtime provisions of the Fair Labor Standards Act (FLSA), earns the same weekly salary regardless of the number of hours worked. Under current FLSA regulations, exempt employees may be suspended for one full day or more for violations of written policies that are applicable to all employees, such as policies regarding sexual harassment or workplace violence.

Union Representation

If employees covered under a collective bargaining agreement believe that meeting with a supervisor or being questioned during an investigation may result in disciplinary action against them, they have the right to a representative. This right is called the Weingarten Rule. Union employees have the right to request a union delegate.

The supervisor does not need to provide a representative; however, the employee should be afforded a reasonable time to obtain one. Union delegates should be required to sign warning notices issued to employees whom they represent. There is a wealth of further information available regarding employees' rights during an investigatory interview.

Tips for Successful Discipline

Do not speak to employees out in the open. Employees deserve to be afforded privacy when they are being counseled. Regardless of the infraction, employees do not deserve to be embarrassed. Follow the adage, "Praise in public; punish in private!"

Managers should maintain a professional, calm demeanor and be firm, but speak to employees with the respect that they deserve.

Managers who come across a situation that will necessitate counseling an employee, and of which proof will be needed later on (for example, a dirty area that the employee was supposed to have cleaned, or an employee who is missing from his assigned work area), should contact a union delegate or some other person to witness the session.

Unless the severity of the incident dictates severe discipline, do not skip the normal steps. Doing so usually results in the perception that the employer was looking to expedite the employee's termination. Each case should be evaluated individually.

In all situations, if an employee is a union member, ask if she requests a delegate. Although it is not legally required, this practice demonstrates goodwill. If the employee declines, the employee should sign a statement that she refused a delegate.

Give the employee a *reasonable* time to seek out a delegate. In a situation in which there is imminent danger, such as threatening or fighting, the employee should be told to punch out, leave the premises, and contact the department to arrange for a meeting, to which he can bring a delegate.

Remember that the notice is called a warning notice because the employer is trying to help employees correct the behavior that is getting them in trouble. Employers don't write people up to get them fired, nor is it most employees' overall objective to get fired.

Employees fire themselves. They begin their employment with perfect performance and a perfect attendance record. As they deviate from that model, they are counseled, then warned, and then suspended. If they choose to ignore these warning signs, they will have fired themselves. The bottom line is: *Firing should never be a surprise for the employee.*

Sometimes managers hesitate to write employees up because of emotional factors. Usually, however, if a problem is ignored, it doesn't go away; it gets worse. An employer is actually doing employees a disservice by ignoring their behavior, making excuses for it, or being overly sympathetic.

Employees appreciate knowing where they stand. One of the worst scenarios is a supervisor who fails to write up an employee, who, in turn, continues to think there's nothing wrong. Then, one day, the supervisor can't take it anymore and emits a frustrated, "*You're fired!*"

Untruthful performance feedback can also have significant legal ramifications. Discipline should always be consistent with business necessity. Warning notices should document the business reasons for addressing the issue.

These tips should help to alleviate some of the apprehension associated with the process of disciplining employees, as well as to build the necessary foundation for surviving the inevitable disciplinary grievances.

REDUCTIONS IN FORCE, THE WARN ACT, AND COBRA

Reduction in Force

An organization must use reduction in force (RIF) procedures when one or more employees will be separated for a reason such as reorganization, lack of work, or shortage of funds. A leave of more than 30 calendar days or of more than 22 discontinuous days is also a RIF action.

RIF is the last resort in downsizing an organization. Because it has an adverse effect on employees and productivity, it is the last option that an organization should pursue when reorganizing or dealing with budget cuts.

Other options that should be considered prior to a RIF are hiring freezes, early retirement, buyouts, and directed reassignments; these should be tried before an organization resorts to a RIF.

To be considered a RIF, separation of an employee must be caused by:

➤ Lack of work
➤ Shortage of funds

- Insufficient personnel ceiling
- Reorganization
- The exercise of reemployment, restoration, or return rights
- Reclassification of an employee's position as a result of erosion of duties when such action will take effect after the organization has formally announced a RIF and the RIF will take effect within 180 days

RIF procedures are required when both the action to be taken and the cause of the action meet these criteria. There are almost always some unexpected and undesirable consequences from a RIF. Examples of these might include:

- Temporary loss of organizational productivity because many people are moving into new, unfamiliar jobs at the same time
- Low employee morale
- High one-time costs in unemployment compensation, lump-sum payments for accrued annual leave, severance pay, and/or continuation of health benefits

More information pertaining to RIFs may be found at the U.S. Office of Personnel Management web site, www.opm.gov/employ/html/RESTRUCT.HTM.

The U.S. Office of Personnel Management offers services to federal agencies to help them meet their human resources needs. While these services are available only to federal agencies, the information provided at the site should be helpful to any organization undertaking a reduction in its workforce.

It can help agencies that are downsizing their workforces in an effective and sensitive manner by offering services that include a comprehensive downsizing plan, technical assistance in RIF planning and execution, development of an outplacement program, career center design, and individual career counseling. This site has detailed information on the downsizing services offered by the U.S. Office of Personnel Management.

Worker Adjustment and Retraining Notification Act

The Worker Adjustment and Retraining Notification (WARN) Act was enacted on August 4, 1988, and became effective on February 4, 1989. The WARN Act provides protection to employees, their families, and communities by requiring employers to give affected employees written notice at least 60 days in advance of any plant closing or mass layoff.

Advance notice gives employees and their families some transition time to adjust to the expected loss of employment, to seek and obtain alternative jobs, and, if necessary, to enter skill training or retraining that will allow them to compete successfully in the job market.

The WARN Act also provides for notice to state dislocated worker units so that dislocated worker assistance can be promptly provided, and to local elected officials so that they may prepare a community response.

Not all plant closings and mass layoffs are subject to the WARN Act, and certain employment circumstances must take place before the WARN Act applies to a particular organization. The WARN Act sets out specific exemptions and provides for a reduction in the notification period in particular circumstances. Damages and civil penalties can be assessed against employers who violate the WARN Act.

Consult a labor attorney before taking any action involving layoffs, shutdowns, or mergers, just to make sure that all legal aspects of those events are handled properly.

Who Is Covered? Generally, employers that have 100 or more employees, not counting employees who have worked less than 6 months in the last 12 months and not counting employees who work an average of less than 20 hours a week, are covered by the WARN Act.

Regular federal, state, and local government entities that provide public services are not covered. Employees entitled to notice under WARN include hourly and salaried workers, and also managerial and supervisory employees.

When Does the WARN Act Apply? The WARN Act generally applies to most plant closings and mass layoffs. WARN defines a plant closing as a shutdown, either temporary or permanent, of an entire single employment site or one or more facilities or operating units within a single employment site. The act applies to any shutdown that results in the termination of employment or layoff for more than 6 months of 50 or more full-time employees during any 30-day period.

WARN defines a mass layoff as a reduction in force, not a plant closing, during any 30-day period that results in the employment loss at a single employment site of either:

> 50 or more full-time employees, if they represent 33 percent of the workforce at the employment site, *or*
> 500 or more full-time employees

Under this definition, a reduction in the workforce of 499 or fewer full-time workers is not a mass layoff if the number of workers does not equal 33 percent of the workforce at that single employment site.

However, a reduction in force of at least 500 full-time workers constitutes a mass layoff, even if the number of employees affected does not represent 33 percent of the workforce at that single employment site.

Part-time employees are excluded from the calculations in a mass layoff situation.

What Is Employment Loss? The term *employment loss* is defined as a termination of employment other than a discharge for cause, retirement, or voluntary separation; or a layoff exceeding 6 months; or a reduction in work hours equal to 50 percent during each month of any 6-month period.

In situations involving relocations or mergers, employment loss may or may not be considered employment loss under the WARN Act.

Under the WARN Act, employment loss excludes a plant closing or layoff resulting from the relocation and consolidation of all or part of the business if:

> Prior to the closing or layoff, the employer offers to transfer the employee to a different site of employment within a reasonable commuting distance with no more than a six-month break in employment; *or*
> The employer offers to transfer the employee to any other site of employment regardless of the distance with no more than a six-month break in employment, and the employee accepts within 30 days of the offer or of the closing or layoff, whichever is later.

Exceptions to the WARN Act. The WARN Act identifies situations in which either no notice is required or less than a 60-day notice is necessary. These situations are unusual in nature and can get complicated from a practical and legal perspective, so consult an employment law attorney before taking any action.

The act explicitly identifies two situations in which no notice is required. These are:

> *Temporary facilities and undertakings of limited duration.* Closings of temporary facilities and layoffs or closings resulting from the completion of a specific undertaking or project are explicitly exempted from the WARN Act. This exemption applies only if the affected workers were hired with the understanding that their employment was limited to the duration of the facility, project, or undertaking.
> *Strikes and lockouts.* A layoff or closing that amounts to a strike or a lockout is not subject to the provisions of the WARN Act unless the strike or lockout results from an effort to avoid the WARN Act's requirements. An employer need not provide notice of a layoff or closing when permanently replacing an employee who is considered to be an economic striker under the National Labor Relations Act.

The WARN Act also specifies three situations in which the 60-day notice requirement may be reduced.

Natural disasters. No 60-day notice is required if the causing event results from a natural disaster, such as a flood, earthquake, or drought. However, the WARN Act also states that notice shall be given as early as practicable under the circumstances, along with a brief statement explaining why less than a 60-day notice is being given.

Unforeseen business circumstances. The notice period requirement can also be reduced if the causing event is an outcome of business circumstances that were not reasonably foreseeable as of the time that notice would have been required. Here too, the WARN Act requires notice as early as practicable along with a brief statement explaining why less than a 60-day notice is being given.

Faltering company. The 60-day notice period requirement can also be reduced for plant closings (but not for mass layoffs) by what is called the faltering company exception.

A faltering company is defined as a company that, at the time notice is required, is actively seeking capital or business that, if obtained, would enable the company to avoid or postpone the causing event and the company reasonably and in good faith believes that giving notice would hinder the company in obtaining the needed capital or business.

Again, the WARN Act requires notice as early as practicable along with a brief statement explaining why less than a 60-day notice is being given.

Notice Required Upon the Sale of a Business. In the case of the sale of all or part of a business, the seller is responsible for communicating any notice for any mass layoff or plant closing up to and including the date of the sale.

After the date of the sale, the purchaser is responsible for communicating any notice under the WARN Act. The WARN Act establishes that a person who is an employee of the seller, other than a part-time employee, as of the date of the sale is considered to be an employee of the purchaser immediately after the date of the sale.

The Consolidated Omnibus Budget Reconciliation Act

The Consolidated Omnibus Budget Reconciliation Act (COBRA) was enacted in 1985 and has undergone several amendments over the years. Again, consult with your certified benefits consultant or legal counsel for the latest requirements.

COBRA mandates that most employers offer a continuation of group health-care coverage to plan participants and certain family members for 18 or 36 months, at group rates, in situations where coverage might otherwise end, such as with a voluntary or involuntary termination of employment, a reduction in the number of hours worked, the death of an employee, or a divorce.

The law generally covers group health plans maintained by employers with 20 or more employees in the prior year. It applies to plans in the private sector and those sponsored by state and local governments. The law does not, however, apply to plans sponsored by the federal government and certain church-related organizations.

Who Is Entitled to Benefits Under COBRA? There are three elements needed to qualify for COBRA benefits. COBRA establishes specific criteria for plans, qualified beneficiaries, and qualifying events.

Plan Coverage

Group health plans for employers with 20 or more employees on more than 50 percent of the typical business days in the previous calendar year are subject to COBRA. Both full- and part-time employees are counted to determine whether a plan is subject to COBRA. Each part-time employee counts as a fraction of an employee, with the fraction equal to the number of hours that the part-time employee worked divided by the number of hours that an employee must work to be considered full time.

Qualified Beneficiaries

A *qualified beneficiary* generally is an individual who is an employee, the employee's spouse, or the employee's dependent child, who was covered by a group health plan on the day before a qualifying event. In certain cases, a retired employee, the retired employee's spouse, and the retired employee's dependent children may be qualified beneficiaries.

In addition, any child born to or placed for adoption with a covered employee during the period of COBRA coverage is considered a qualified beneficiary. Agents, independent contractors, and directors who participate in the group health plan may also be qualified beneficiaries.

Qualifying Events

Qualifying events are particular events that would cause an individual to lose health coverage. The type of qualifying event will determine who the qualified beneficiaries are and the amount of time that a plan must offer the health coverage to them under COBRA. A plan, at its discretion, may provide longer periods of continuation coverage.

The qualifying events for *employees* are:

> - Voluntary or involuntary termination of employment for reasons other than "gross misconduct"
> - Reduction in the number of hours of employment
>   The qualifying events for *spouses* are:
> - Voluntary or involuntary termination of the covered employee's employment for any reason other than "gross misconduct"
> - Reduction in the hours worked by the covered employee
> - The covered employee's becoming entitled to Medicare
> - Divorce or legal separation of the covered employee
> - Death of the covered employee

The qualifying events for *dependent children* are the same as those for the spouse, with one addition:

> - Loss of "dependent child" status under the plan rules

How Does a Person Become Eligible for COBRA Continuation Coverage? To be eligible for COBRA coverage, you must have been enrolled in your employer's health plan when you worked, and the health plan must continue to be in effect for active employees.

COBRA continuation coverage is available upon the occurrence of a qualifying event that would, except for the COBRA continuation coverage, cause an individual to lose her health-care coverage.

What Process Must Individuals Follow to Elect COBRA Continuation Coverage?
Employers must notify plan administrators of a qualifying event within 30 days after an employee's death, termination, reduced hours of employment, or entitlement to Medicare.

A qualified beneficiary must notify the plan administrator of a qualifying event within 60 days after divorce or legal separation or a child's ceasing to be covered as a dependent under plan rules.

Plan participants and beneficiaries generally must be sent an election notice not later than 14 days after the plan administrator receives notice that a qualifying event has occurred. The individual then has 60 days to decide whether to elect COBRA continuation coverage. The person has 45 days after electing coverage to pay the initial premium.

How Do I File a COBRA Claim for Benefits?
Health plan rules must explain how to obtain benefits and must include written procedures for processing claims. Claims procedures must be described in the Summary Plan Description.

You should submit a claim for benefits in accordance with the plan's rules for filing claims. If the claim is denied, you must be given notice of the denial in writing, generally within 90 days after the claim is filed. The notice should state the reasons for the denial, any additional information needed to support the claim, and procedures for appealing the denial.

You will have at least 60 days to appeal a denial, and generally you must receive a decision on the appeal within 60 days after that. Contact the plan administrator for more information on filing a claim for benefits. Complete plan rules are available from your employer or benefits office. There can be charges of up to 25 cents a page for copies of plan rules.

Can Individuals Qualify for Longer Periods of COBRA Continuation Coverage?
Yes; disability can extend the 18-month period of continuation coverage for a qualifying event that is a termination of employment or reduction of hours. To qualify for additional months of COBRA continuation coverage, the qualified beneficiary must:

- Have a ruling from the Social Security Administration that he became disabled within the first 60 days of COBRA continuation coverage
- Send the plan a copy of the Social Security ruling letter within 60 days of receipt, but prior to expiration of the 18-month period of coverage.

If these requirements are met, the entire family qualifies for an additional 11 months of COBRA continuation coverage. Plans can charge 150 percent of the premium cost for the extended period of coverage.

Is a Divorced Spouse Entitled to COBRA Coverage From the Former Spouse's Group Health Plan?

Under COBRA, participants, covered spouses, and dependent children may continue their plan coverage for a limited time when they would otherwise lose coverage as a result of a particular event, such as divorce (or legal separation).

A covered employee's spouse who would lose coverage as a result of a divorce may elect continuation coverage under the plan for a maximum of 36 months. A qualified beneficiary must notify the plan administrator of a qualifying event within 60 days after divorce or legal separation.

After being notified of a divorce, the plan administrator must give notice, generally within 14 days, to the qualified beneficiary of the right to elect COBRA continuation coverage. Divorced spouses may call their plan administrator or the nearest Pension and Welfare Benefits Administration regional office if they have questions about COBRA continuation coverage.

Under COBRA, What Benefits Must Be Provided?

Qualified beneficiaries must be offered the same coverage that they had right before they qualified for continuation coverage. A change in the benefits under the plan for the active employees will also apply to qualified beneficiaries.

Qualified beneficiaries must be allowed to make the same choices given to non-COBRA beneficiaries under the plan, such as during periods of open enrollment by the plan.

When Does COBRA Coverage Begin?

COBRA coverage begins on the date that health-care coverage would otherwise have been lost by reason of a qualifying event.

How Long Does COBRA Coverage Last?

COBRA establishes required periods of coverage for continuation health benefits. A plan, however, may provide longer periods of coverage than those required by COBRA. COBRA beneficiaries generally are eligible for group coverage for a maximum of 18 months for qualifying events involving employment termination or reduction in hours of work.

Certain qualifying events, or a second qualifying event during the initial period of coverage, may permit a beneficiary to receive a maximum of 36 months of coverage. Coverage begins on the date that coverage would otherwise have been lost by reason of a qualifying event and will end at the end of the maximum period. It may end earlier if:

> Premiums are not paid on a timely basis.
> The employer ceases to maintain any group health plan.
> After the COBRA election, coverage is obtained through another employer group health plan that does not contain any exclusion or limitation with respect to any preexisting condition of such beneficiary.

However, if other group health coverage is obtained prior to the COBRA election, COBRA coverage may not be discontinued, even if the other coverage continues after the COBRA election.

> After the COBRA election, a beneficiary becomes entitled to Medicare benefits. However, if Medicare is obtained prior to the COBRA election, COBRA coverage may not be discontinued, even if the Medicare coverage continues after the COBRA election.

Although COBRA specifies certain periods of time during which continuation health coverage must be offered to qualified beneficiaries, COBRA does not prohibit plans from offering continuation health coverage that goes beyond the COBRA periods.

Some plans allow participants and beneficiaries to convert group health coverage to an individual policy. If this option is generally available from the plan, a qualified beneficiary who pays for COBRA coverage must be given the option of converting to an individual policy at the end of the COBRA continuation coverage period.

The option to enroll in a conversion health plan must be offered within 180 days before COBRA coverage ends. The premium for a conversion policy may be more expensive than the premium of a group plan, and the conversion policy may provide a lower level of coverage.

The conversion option, however, is not available if the beneficiary ends COBRA coverage before reaching the end of the maximum period of COBRA coverage.

If I Elect COBRA, How Much Do I Pay? When you were an active employee, your employer may have paid all or part of your group health premiums. Under COBRA, as a former employee who is no longer receiving benefits, you will usually pay the entire premium amount, that is, the portion of the premium that you paid as an active employee and the amount of the contribution made by your employer. In addition, there may be a 2 percent administrative fee.

While COBRA rates may seem high, you will be paying group premium rates, which are usually lower than individual rates. Since it is likely that there will be a lapse of a month or more between the date of your layoff and the time you make the COBRA election decision, you may have to pay health premiums retroactively from the time of your separation from the company.

The first premium, for instance, will cover the entire time since your last day of employment with your former employer. You should also be aware that it is your responsibility to pay for COBRA coverage, even if you do not receive a monthly statement. Although they are not required to do so, some employers may subsidize COBRA coverage.

Where Can I Get More Information on COBRA? COBRA administration is shared by three federal agencies. The Departments of Labor and Treasury have jurisdiction over private-sector group health plans. The Department of Health and Human Services administers the continuation coverage law as it affects public-sector health plans.

EXIT PROCEDURES

We've done everything by the book so far, but we will still have the occasional quit or termination. This is when we have a parting of the ways. It may be initiated by either the employee or the employer. Exit procedures are necessary and valuable, whether the reason for ending the employee-employer relationship is a termination, resignation, retirement, or any other reason.

The Exit Interview

Basically, an exit interview has three purposes:

1. To learn where the organization can improve itself
2. To make sure that employees leave feeling as good as they can about their experience
3. In some cases, to encourage the employee to stay under new circumstances

The information collected in an exit interview can give an organization a unique perspective on its performance and employee satisfaction and how they compare with those at other employers.

An exit interview should be an accepted expectation of employees. But legally, employers don't have a leg to stand on if an employee refuses. To encourage more employees to participate in an exit interview, employers should stress the confidentiality of the discussions.

People are sometimes nervous about saying too much and possibly burning their bridges. They rely on former managers and team members for references and networking. One of the worst experiences we've seen arose from an exit interview where bad behavior by a manager had to be reported. Those comments got back to him almost immediately, and he openly lost his temper in the office. It chilled the entire workplace.

Inform all departing employees that their comments will be scrubbed of identifying information before they are shared with anyone in the office, with some exceptions. If the employee reports criminal behavior, sexual harassment, incidents of discrimination, or other legal issues, you have an obligation to take action.

Encourage employees to be as honest as they can, and explain that the point is to learn what we do well and what we can do better to keep our clients and staff happy.

Assuring confidentiality might be more difficult for small employers and those with low turnover because the sources of the information may be obvious. While there's not much that an employer can do to guarantee confidentiality, employees should be told how the information they give will be used, and that the organization will make every effort to take action in a way that doesn't compromise them.

By their nature, exit interviews can become either too confrontational or too perfunctory, so the interviewer must be extremely experienced and skilled to gently probe for the full truth. And if an interviewer is not trained in active listening or is not strongly empathetic, she is likely to take offense if the employee starts to vent. This can be a very emotional encounter, and the interviewer needs to be able to manage it skillfully.

The interviewer needn't necessarily be an HR professional. A neutral manager or mentor whom the employee trusts and who has good interviewing skills could be the right choice. Outsourcing the exit interview to an independent third party is also a good choice. The only real disadvantage to employers might be the cost. You have a higher probability of getting a trained interviewer, the interviewer can gather systematic data, and employees are more likely to be honest and cooperative.

Exit interviews must have a mechanism for capturing the information gleaned. Just as when you are interviewing a candidate, you're better off having a structured process that allows you to capture information that can be compared and analyzed.

The degree of structure can range from a casual conversation with note taking to a standardized list of talking points to a questionnaire or other survey instrument. However, relying on a casual conversation generally does not provide consistent feedback that can be compiled and compared, not to mention the risk involved in allowing an unskilled interviewer to just "wing it."

Ideally, the interviewer should have a structured plan, but should carry it out in the context of a casual conversation. In other words, instead of just reading a bunch of cold questions, the interviewer should be familiar enough with the content that he can elicit information without coming across as either a robot or an interrogator.

Just as an aside, there are some people who believe that you can get better information if you wait until after the employee's departure, and then send a questionnaire (by mail or e-mail) that the employee complete on her own, at her convenience. Yet another option is to use a third-party telephone interview. However, for the purposes of this kit, we will provide the tools and information to do it yourself. So, let's go!

There are two basic scenarios that need to be considered. The first is when the employee initiates the departure, and the employer would like him to stay. That is *negative turnover*. It is negative because it has a negative effect on the organization, and it wasn't your choice.

These people may be brutally honest about their experiences without fear of immediate repercussions. In addition, it's likely that they have recently been job hunting and interviewing and can offer some useful intelligence on how the organization compares with other employers, and why they believe that the grass will be greener on the other side of the fence.

Then there is the situation in which the organization makes the decision to terminate someone's employment, or the employee decides to leave on her own, but she was not a viable long-term employee, and it is best for the organization that she leave. That is *positive turnover*. It is positive because the result will be positive for the employer, and either way, the employee needed to go.

Regardless of whether the exit is a termination or a resignation, there are some common procedures that all organizations need to follow in addition to the exit interview, such as:

➢   Return of organization property, keys, access cards, and so on
➢   Review and acknowledgment of any agreements, such as confidentiality, non-compete, and so on
➢   Benefits forms and disclosures—COBRA, 401(k), and so on

Negative Turnover

Before we dive into how to handle the departure of a valuable employee, we recommend that you go back to the "Creative Sourcing Strategies" section of Chapter 2 and review the boomerang strategies. This section already explained how to orchestrate the exit in a positive and productive way that leaves the door open for, and gives the employee incentives for, his return.

So rather than go through all of that again, just be sure that you keep your hooks in the employee with the goal of getting her back. That includes the "Get

Out of Jail Free" card, staying in touch, a delayed exit interview, and other such techniques.

The only thing left to cover here is the actual exit interview, which normally occurs during the last day or week of the person's employment. The questions and information that you want to cover are a little different for someone you wanted to have stay than they are for someone you are terminating, or who you are glad is resigning.

See the templates at the end of this section (and on the enclosed CD).

Positive Turnover

As mentioned before, positive turnover occurs when someone leaves the organization, either voluntarily or involuntarily, who just wasn't a good fit either for the job or for the organization.

If you have implemented the other concepts in this kit, these people should be few and far between, especially if you are using the behavioral assessment tools to ensure a better person-job match.

Even then, there will be the occasional times when the marriage just doesn't work. However, if you find this occurring more often than it should (do the math), then you need to go back and look at your recruitment, selection, and retention processes to see where you may need to retool. Going back and repeating the HR Self-Assessment might also prove valuable.

Did you not follow your own selection process? Did you ignore the signs warning you against the hiring decision (person-job match, red flags in the interview, accurate and up-to-date job description/success profile, training, performance management, and so on)? These questions need to be answered so that you don't find yourself back in the revolving-door scenario that this whole kit was supposed to be fixing.

Next, you need to handle the exit in an effective and professional manner. Even though you don't want this person back, he is still going to be talking about you in the community. Even though this is a negative process, you can leave a positive last impression as he goes out the door. *For the last time, HR is PR!*

If the person is resigning voluntarily, the process is a little less onerous and ominous. Wish him well, acknowledge his desire to pursue other opportunities, and close the book. However, if you are initiating the termination, the scenario is a little more tenuous and challenging.

Clearly the termination should not come as a surprise or a shock if you have been utilizing the performance management tools and techniques recommended in this kit. However, it is never easy to make and communicate this final decision.

Ideally, if the person does not have another job opportunity already lined up (which is usually the case), consider offering the employee the services of an outplacement firm. These firms will actually come on-site to talk with the person immediately after she has been given the bad news, and then work with her for a period of time to get her focused on the future, and hopefully gainfully employed as soon as possible.

One of the most important functions of the outplacement specialist is to give the person some firm and immediate dos and don'ts and keep her engaged in productive and positive behavior in the days immediately following her termination.

At first blush, this may appear to be an unnecessary expense, but consider it cheap insurance to accomplish the following:

- It leaves the most positive last impression possible, to prevent the person from bad-mouthing you in the community, and communicates to the rest of your organization that you are a compassionate employer, even during a termination.
- It prevents the employee from doing something stupid or harmful to himself or to others (e.g., getting drunk, going on vacation, not telling his spouse, turning his rage into action, and so on).
- It reduces or eliminates your potential unemployment compensation liability, since the person is likely to become reemployed much sooner than if he were just left to his own devices.

On the following pages are a variety of checklists and questionnaires and a termination letter form that you can tailor to your own organization's needs. All of these forms are also on the enclosed CD.

EXIT CHECKLIST 1

Name: _____ Department: _____

Manager: _____ Termination Date: _____ Hire Date: _____

Forwarding Address: _____

Exit Interview
☐ Interviewed   Date: _____ By: _____
☐ Questionnaire and Synopsis Reviewed and Filed   Date: _____

Returned
☐ Keys: _____   Date: _____
☐ I.D. Card: _____   Date: _____

Payroll
☐ Final Paycheck: Amount: _____   Date: _____
☐ Severance: Amount: _____   Date: _____
☐ Vacation: Days: _____   Amount: _____   Date: _____
☐ Terminated in System   Amount: _____   Date: _____   ☐ AutoPay Off
Eligible for Rehire?   Yes ☐   No ☐   Reason: _____

Benefits
☐ COBRA & HIPPA explained   ☐ Health Terminated   ☐ 401(k) Terminated
COBRA Notification Deadline: _____   COBRA Notification Date: _____

Cancelled or Transferred
☐ Memberships: _____   Date: _____
☐ Periodicals: _____   Date: _____
Verified By: _____   Date: _____

EXIT CHECKLIST 2

Employee Information

Employee Name   Employee Number   Term Date

If termination is involuntary
☐ Documentation of performance issues and disciplinary action is in employee file.

Before employee's last day of employment

Human Resources

☐ Prepare COBRA letter

☐ Schedule exit interview

☐ Cancel stock options

   ☐ Final expense reports submitted.

   ☐ Final expense reports paid.

Accounting/Finance

☐ Final paycheck is being prepared.

☐ Check for final balances on
corporate credit card and cancel card.

Office Coordinator/Facilities

☐ Cancel voicemail account effective employee's last day.

☐ Request to have employee's network access closed effective employee's last day.

Last day of employment

☐ Provide COBRA letter and explain

- 60 days to elect coverage
- 45 days to send in premium for all
months since coverage ceased
- Premium due 1st of the month

☐ Non-disclosure agreement

- Provide copy
- Explain non-compete
- Retrieve any confidential information

☐ Vested stock options

- 90 days to submit the form to exercise.

☐ Last paycheck (please check one)

   ☐ Provided at exit interview *or*

   ☐ Mailed after termination date

☐ Provide 401(k) withdrawal form

☐ Address changes verified

☐ Collect or verify computer
system(s) or equipment

☐ Collect security card

☐ Collect cell phone

☐ Collect phone card

☐ Collect corporate credit card

☐ Exit interview questionnaire

☐ Departure is communicated to staff

☐ Eligible for rehire?

   Yes_____ No _____

☐ Terminate status in the HRIS system

After the employee's last day

☐ Check for any additional amounts owed for commissions, expense reports, etc.

☐ Mail final pay stub to former employee if necessary.

☐ Complete and submit benefit forms to stop coverage with Aetna and Fortis.

☐ If former employee submits a request for COBRA coverage, reenroll using Aetna enrollment
forms. (Refer to COBRA process document.)

Reason for leaving

_____

_____

Employee Signature   Date

Exit Interview Questionnaire 1: Voluntary Quit

Employee_____   Employee No. _____

Manager _____   Department _____

Termination Date _____   Last Day at Work _____

On your leaving the company, we want to provide an opportunity for you to comment on your reason for leaving, and to recommend any changes to the organization that you feel appropriate. Please complete this form as preparation for our discussion.

1. Were your initial objectives for joining Company XYZ met? Please elaborate on how they were met or how they may have changed.

_____

_____

_____

2. What aspects of your job were the most satisfying?

_____

_____

_____

3. Suggest any specific changes that would have kept you at Company XYZ.

_____

_____

_____

4. Recommend any changes you would like to suggest that you feel would benefit:

   A. The organization _____

   _____

   B. Your department _____

   _____

   C. Other employees _____

   _____

5. Is there a point of uncertainty or disagreement that you've been unable to settle satisfactorily that you would like to discuss?

   _____

   _____

   _____

6. Please comment on your reason for leaving Company XYZ.

   _____

   _____

   _____

7. Please comment on the Employee Benefit Plan. Did it meet your needs sufficiently? Was your compensation sufficient in recognizing your performance?

   _____

   _____

   _____

8. Discuss briefly your new responsibilities.

   _____

   _____

   _____

9. Any additional comments are welcome.

   _____

   _____

   _____

   _____

Exit Interview Questionnaire 2: Voluntary Quit

We would appreciate you taking about 8 to 10 minutes to answer the following questions as honestly as possible. Your individual responses are treated as confidential and will not become part of your personnel file.

We believe that the information is of vital importance and will assist us in analyzing our employee retention and turnover. Thank you for your cooperation!

Name _____   Employment Date _____

Department _____   Termination Date _____

Position _____   Manager _____

What prompted you to seek alternative employment?

☐ Type of Work   ☐ Quality of Supervision

☐ Compensation   ☐ Work Conditions

☐ Lack of Recognition   ☐ Family Circumstances

☐ Organization Culture   ☐ Career Advancement Opportunity

☐ Business/Product Direction   ☐ Other: _____

Before making your decision to leave, did you investigate other options that would enable you to stay?

☐ Yes   ☐ No   If "yes," describe: _____

What did you think of your supervision in regard to the following?

	Almost Always	Sometimes	Never	Comments
Demonstrated fair and equal treatment	☐	☐	☐	
Provided recognition on the job	☐	☐	☐	
Developed cooperation and teamwork	☐	☐	☐	
Encouraged/listened to suggestions	☐	☐	☐	
Followed policies and practices	☐	☐	☐	

How would you rate the following in relation to your job?

	Excellent	Good	Fair	Poor	Comments
Cooperation within your department	☐	☐	☐	☐	
Cooperation with other departments	☐	☐	☐	☐	
Communications in your department	☐	☐	☐	☐	
Communications within the organization as a whole	☐	☐	☐	☐	

Communications between you
and your manager   ☐   ☐   ☐   ☐

Morale in your department   ☐   ☐   ☐   ☐

Job satisfaction   ☐   ☐   ☐   ☐

Training you received   ☐   ☐   ☐   ☐

Growth potential   ☐   ☐   ☐   ☐

Was your workload usually:

☐ Too great

☐ Varied, but all right

☐ About right

☐ Too light

How did you feel about your salary and the employee benefits?

	Excellent	Good	Fair	Poor	Comments
Base salary	☐	☐	☐	☐	
Medical plan	☐	☐	☐	☐	
Dental plan	☐	☐	☐	☐	
Vision plan	☐	☐	☐	☐	
401(k) plan	☐	☐	☐	☐	
Life insurance	☐	☐	☐	☐	
Paid time off	☐	☐	☐	☐	
STD/LTD plan	☐	☐	☐	☐	
Stock options	☐	☐	☐	☐	

Are there any other benefits you feel should have been offered?

☐ Yes   ☐ No

If "yes," what?

_____

Any other comments on benefits?

_____

How frequently did you get performance feedback?

_____

_____

What were your feelings about the performance review process?

_____

_____

How frequently did you have discussions with your manager about your career goals?

_____

_____

What did you like most about your job and/or this company?

_____

_____

What did you like least about your job and/or this company?

_____

_____

What does your new job offer that your job with this company does not?

_____

_____

Why is the new job/company better?

_____

_____

Do you have any suggestions for improvement? Have you raised them in the past?

_____

_____

Would you recommend this company to a friend as a place to work?
☐ Yes, without reservations   ☐ Yes, with reservations   ☐ No

Additional comments about your job or this company:

_____

_____

Termination Letter

Dear :

Your last day of employment with {Enter Company Name} was _____. As a terminating employee, there are a number of issues related to your benefits of which you will need to be aware.

_____ Medical and Dental Coverage

You have the option to continue your group medical and dental coverage through the COBRA Plan. All benefits cease on your last working day, unless you elect COBRA coverage. Information on COBRA will be sent to you shortly by certified mail. If you terminate employment in the first half of the month, you will receive credit for the last half of the month's premium if paid. If you terminate during the last half of the month, no credit will be given.

_____ Group Term Life Insurance

Your coverage ceases on your termination date; however, you have the option to convert your group term life insurance to an individual policy with {Enter Carrier Name} within 31 days following your termination date. If you are interested, please contact me to obtain a conversion form. You will then submit your completed conversion form to a local agent, who will be referred to you by the {Enter Carrier Name} sales office.

_____ Dependent Life Insurance

Your spouse or child dependent life coverage ceases on your termination date; however, you have the option to convert to an individual policy with {Enter Carrier Name} within 31 days following your termination date. If you are interested, please contact me to obtain a conversion form. You will then submit your completed form to a local agent, who will be referred to you by the {Enter Carrier Name} sales office.

_____ Personal Life Insurance

If you have a payroll-deducted personal life insurance plan, you will need to contact your insurance representative, who will assist you in arranging for the premiums to be paid by bank draft.

_____ Long-Term Disability Insurance

Your LTD plan ceases on your termination date; however, you have the option to continue this coverage by making payments directly to the carrier, {Enter Carrier Name}. Contact {Enter Contact Name and Telephone Number}.

_____ Group Long-Term Disability Insurance

Your group plan through {Enter Carrier Name} ceases on your termination date; however, you could convert this coverage to another plan. Contact {Enter Contact Name and Telephone Number}.

_____ Auto/Homeowner's Insurance

You will need to contact {Enter Carrier Name} at {Enter Telephone Number} to make arrangements to continue your insurance. You will no longer be eligible for the group discount that is available through payroll deduction.

_____ Flexible Spending Account

If you have a balance in your flexible spending account when you terminate employment, you may continue to file claims for eligible expenses against the balance until the end of the plan year, {Enter date plan year ends}.

____ **Profit Sharing**

If you have three or more years of service upon termination, you are entitled to benefits from the plan. According to the plan, distribution of benefits is payable at normal retirement age (65) or at termination of service, if later. The Retirement Committee will, however, consider applications for early distribution after one year following termination of employment. Annual statements will be sent to you at your home address. In order to receive an early profit-sharing distribution, requests should be made in writing approximately one year following your termination date to {Enter contact name, address, and telephone number} for an application or if you have questions.

____ **401(k) Plan**

If you have participated in the 401(k) Plan, your benefit will be based on the value of your account, which comprises contributions you have made and any investment earnings/losses. 401(k) distributions are subject to the same rules and regulations as distributions from the Profit-Sharing Plan (see above).

____ **Credit Union**

Although your deductions will cease, you can continue to keep your account open. Contact the {Enter Credit Union Name}.

____ **Separation Notice**

As required by law, a Separation Notice is enclosed.

____ **Pay**

For the pay period ending _____ , you will receive the following:

{Enter Data}

To ensure that you receive documents and notices from the organization, be sure to contact us if your address changes. If you have any questions, please call me at {Enter Telephone Number}.

Sincerely yours,

{Enter Name and Title}

PART 3

LEADERSHIP AND ACTION PLANNING: TURNING INTENTIONS INTO ACTIONS

CHAPTER 15

Transforming Your Management Team Into a Leadership Team

The next and final section of the kit is an action plan that you and your management team can use to keep you on task and create some accountability for implementation.

But before we go there, we need to make a distinction between a *management* team and a *leadership* team. You may have noticed that up to now, we have used these terms somewhat interchangeably. However, they are not the same.

People in most organizations have some sort of periodic meeting with their managers. Unfortunately, these meetings are usually a combination of information dump and butt-kicking. That's management. The word *management* is rooted in the Latin *manus*, which means "to handle."

If you are going to truly adopt any or all of the recommendations in this kit, you need to progress from a management mentality to a leadership mindset. What does that mean?

One of the common characteristics of successful organizations is that they have good communication between departments. And an integral part of that communication is regular, formal, well-structured management and leadership team meetings.

The distinction between a management team meeting and a leadership team meeting is that managing implies a more day-to-day operational perspective (current sales, inventories, last month's numbers, and so on), as opposed to leading, which implies a more forward-thinking, strategic focus (process improvement, best practices, professional development, and so on).

Following are some guidelines for beginning the process of conducting effective leadership team meetings.

TOP 10 GUIDELINES FOR CONDUCTING EFFECTIVE LEADERSHIP TEAM MEETINGS

1. *Establish a standard day, time, and location.* Make these meetings a habit, such as every Tuesday at 8:00 A.M. at Joe's Restaurant in the private room. Yes, these meetings tend to be more effective if they can be held offsite. They can even be held at someone's home. If this is not an option, then be sure that there are no distractions or interruptions. Cell phones off. Door closed with a sign that says, "Meeting in Progress—Do Not Interrupt Unless It Is an Emergency!"

2. *Make the meetings mandatory.* Participating in leadership team meetings is part of a manager's job description. Nothing short of death, disability, or a vacation should take a higher priority. The senior managers should take and track attendance, note in people's personnel files how many meetings each attended, and incorporate this information into performance reviews and reward decisions.

3. *Have an agenda.* It can even be a template, as long as it is followed. Having an agenda keeps the team focused, on track, and on schedule. (A sample agenda is given in the next section and on the CD.)

4. *Take notes.* Ideally, take turns assigning someone to be the recorder. It is less burdensome that way. Always use an Action Plan (see the back of the kit and the CD) that is a living, evolving document. Record the results of the discussion of each agenda item, along with who is responsible for taking any actions, and when these actions are to be completed. Then distribute the minutes and the Action Plan

to everyone as soon as possible after the meeting. This will become the first agenda item at the next meeting.

5. *Start on time and end on time.* Starting on time is more important than ending on time because it sets a standard and an expectation. When you wait for latecomers or review what they missed, you are rewarding tardiness and punishing promptness. Ending on time is important, so that these meetings do not become drudgery. If you are really on a roll or in a creative zone, there is nothing wrong with extending the meeting, but only with the permission of the attendees (i.e., they may have something else pressing back at the organization).

6. *Everyone participates; no one dominates.* As the team leader, you must learn to be aware of the dynamics of the group. There will usually be stronger and weaker participants, but that doesn't mean that they don't all have something valuable to contribute. Use a "round-robin" technique, where you call on each person, one at a time, for input, perspective, or other information on each agenda item.

7. *Always have at least one strategic initiative in process.* As was mentioned in the introduction, leadership implies being strategic. It is fine and necessary to discuss operational issues and challenges, but always be working on at least one forward-thinking process improvement initiative, as well.

8. *Bring in outsiders (on occasion).* Whether it's an employee who might have fresh perspectives or input on an initiative or someone from outside the organization who can share his success or ideas, perhaps even from another industry, this can help get your creative juices flowing.

9. *Work for food.* For some reason, meetings seem to go better when food and beverages are provided. Whether it's the little perk, or whether it's that people loosen up more when they are sharing food and drinks, it does make meetings more palatable (pun intended). It doesn't have to be lobster and filet. Just coffee and donuts in the morning, or end the meeting with a pizza lunch. Just don't let the food and drink become more important than the agenda.

10. *Celebrate success.* When someone achieves a milestone or the organization has a win, be sure to celebrate. All work and no play makes a leadership team go away!

Sample Leadership Team Agenda

I. Attendance

II. Operational review

    A. Round-robin departmental reports (5 minutes each)

        1. Performance metrics

        2. Upcoming activities (special events, VIP visitors, big sale, and so on)

        3. Challenges

        4. Successes

III. Strategic initiatives

    A. Review of minutes and Action Plan from last meeting

    B. Review progress for each person who was assigned an action at the prior meeting

    C. Update and reassign actions, as appropriate

IV. Optional training component

    A. Video, book review, or some other motivational or skill-building module

V. New business

    A. Open forum to ideas for future discussion or action

    B. Add to Action Plan or table for future discussion

HR ACTION PLAN

What follows is a simple document that you should use at every management and leadership team meeting. Make it a requirement for everyone to bring the latest copy, along with their progress reports.

Your team should put whatever action item you are working on in the "What" column, and then indicate "Who" is accountable for each item, as well as a deadline "By When." The only column that should change from week to week is "Status Notes," where the person or people in the "Who" column can update the team on their progress (or lack thereof).

The beauty of this Action Plan is that it keeps everyone on target, on the same page, and on task. Even more important, it holds people accountable. No one wants to come to the leadership team meeting and be embarrassed because she did not deliver the goods. We call this the "cringe factor." If someone has to cringe enough times, that person will eventually either deliver or be delivered up.

[Your Organization's] HR Action Plan

Today's Date:

What	Who	By When	Status Notes
HR Self-Assessment			
"Why Work Here?" Statement			
Bird-Dog Policy			
Recruitment Brochure			
Web Site			
Behavioral Assessment and Selection Tools			
Business Cards for Everyone			
Employee Handbook(s)			
New-Employee Orientation On-Boarding Program			
Creative Recruitment Sources			
Job Descriptions			
Standard Interview Questions			
Boomerang Strategies			
Performance Management			
Employee Perception Survey			

NEXT MEETING:

DATE: _____   TIME: _____   PLACE: _____

TO BE COMPLETED AT END OF EACH MEETING AND DISTRIBUTED TO ALL STAKEHOLDERS

HR STRATEGIC ACTION PLAN (DETAILED)

Following is an example of how to flesh out the Action Plan with specific action steps. You should do the same with whatever items are in your Action Plan. It is important to break the actions into specific steps so that those responsible know what is required of them, and so everyone can see tangible progress along the way.

I. **HR Self-Assessment**
   A. Have the entire leadership team complete it (it takes 10 minutes maximum).
   B. Identify strengths (save them for "Why Work Here?" brochure, web site, etc.).
   C. Identify areas of opportunity (OK, weaknesses).
      1. Pick one area at a time to work on as a leadership team; add to agenda.

II. **"Why Work Here?" Statement**
   A. Refer to strengths from HR Self-Assessment.
   B. Solicit others from the leadership team.
   C. Interview senior employees.
      1. Get quotes and pictures for recruitment brochure, web site.
   D. Have each member of the leadership team draft his version (one paragraph).
   E. Regroup, read each one aloud, and craft the final version.

III. **Bird-Dog Policy/Procedure**
   A. Internal *(for staff)*.
      1. How much?
      2. Pay half at hire; other half when? (After 6 months?)
      3. Put in writing.
   B. External *(for all others)*.
      Same as above plus:
      1. Create referral cards: We Pay for Great People!
         a. Policy (how much, when paid, etc.).
         b. "Why Work Here?"

     c. Directions to web site/application form.

     d. Leave place for bird dog to put his/her name.

IV. **Recruitment Brochure**

    A. "Why Work Here?" statement.

    B. Bird-dog policy.

    C. Employee photos and testimonials.

    D. Key benefits.

    E. Awards and accolades.

    F. Pictures of facility.

    G. Web site address—directions to application form.

    H. E-mail address for more info.

     I. Map with directions to facility.

    J. Name and phone number of primary contact for employment.

    K. Equal Opportunity statement.

V. **Web Site**

    A. Import recruitment brochure content into organization web site.

    B. Add application link that automatically e-mails hiring authority.

    C. Set up process for prompt, personal reply (not just auto-respond).

VI. **Behavioral Assessment and Selection Tools**

(Critical *before* you start recruiting)

    A. Call FirStep, Inc. @ 724-TO LEARN (865-3276) or toll free 1-877-HRxHotline (877-479-4685) to get you started.

VII. **Business Cards for Everyone**

    A. Review/revise job titles (when in doubt, use *associate* or *team member*).

    B. Decide whether to produce cards in-house or via a copy house.

    C. If in-house, purchase templates and supplies at local office store.

    D. Design card (logo, colors, content).

    E. Assign person to learn setup and printing process.

    F. "Why Work Here?" statement and bird-dog bonus on back.

    G. "Bird-dog" statement = We Pay for Great People!

    H. Schedule all-employee meeting to distribute business cards.

I. Reannounce "bird-dog" benefit.

J. Hand out business cards (100 per person if done in-house).

    1. Advise how to get more when needed (administrative person).

K. Hand out recruitment brochures (6 per person).

1. Walk through brochure; emphasize positives.

VIII. **Employee Handbook(s)**

    A. Develop values handbook.

    B. Complete official handbook template.

    C. Distribute both handbooks to current employees (all employees at department meetings).

IX. **New-Employee Orientation/On-Boarding Program**

    A. Structure and content.

        1. First impression (make the first day an event).

            a. Cake?

            b. Group welcome?

            c. Logo wear?

            d. Coffee mug? Etc.

        2. Formal process to instill organization values.

            a. Educate in who we are.

            b. Values employee handbook.

        3. Assign a mentor or coach.

        4. Other required steps (actual employee handbook, policies and procedures, job description review, meet staff, and so on).

X. **Creative Recruitment Sources**

    A. Meet and brainstorm best new sources or strategies for recruits.

    B. Get consensus on which one(s) to do first.

        1. Put in Action Plan with specific date(s) and names.

        2. Revisit at each leadership team meeting to keep fresh and active.

XI. **Job Descriptions/Success Profiles**

    A. Start with most frequently filled positions.

    B. Develop own template from CD.

XII. *Standard* **Behavioral Interview Questions** (*based on job descriptions*)

   A. Use Candidate Assessment Form from CD.

   (*Tailored* questions to be developed for each candidate based on résumé, application form, and other candidate-specific sources before each interview.)

XIII. **Boomerang Strategies**

   A. Decide which strategies are right for your organization. Examples:

   1. Get Out of Jail Free cards.

      a. Can use the same templates as business cards.

      b. Should say, "If you ever want to come back to _____ , and we have a job that fits your skills, you are hired!"

   2. Restore/bridge service if return within _____.

   3. Follow-up strategies.

      a. Post-exit interview (meet for coffee, etc.) 3 to 6 months after exit.

      b. Send newsletter or other communications.

   4. Welcome home parties.

      a. Showcase boomerangs returning.

      b. Cake? Group welcome? Etc.

      c. Golden boomerang.

XIV. **Performance Management**

   A. Go back to HR Toolkit and pick one job at a time to develop.

   1. See Performance Review and Development templates.

   B. Establish schedule for conducting reviews.

   C. Get training on how to conduct performance discussions.

   D. Share forms and process with staff (employee meetings recommended).

XV. **Employee Perception Survey**

   A. Go back to HR Toolkit and develop survey.

   B. Follow process detailed in HR Toolkit.

XVI. *Celebrate Successes!*

Conclusion

Well, we hope you made it this far! Just remember, this is a process, not an event. The good news is that you can follow the plan at your own pace, and still see dramatic improvement rather quickly. The other good news is that when you start to see the benefits of implementing the recommendations in this kit, you will be motivated to continue improving your organization's human resources capabilities.

This kit has introduced you to a lot of information, which can be a little overwhelming at first. To be successful in human resources, both strategically and operationally, we like to use the analogy of a bath rather than a vaccination. Becoming an employer of choice requires daily diligence; it's not an annual event.

It's a mindset, not a program. Although a lot of the initiatives in this kit involve processes and forms, the ultimate litmus test is your intentions and motivations for adopting these processes.

For example, your intention for implementing a solid performance management process should have retention and motivation as its primary goal, not just getting your ducks in a row to terminate someone.

Or, your motivation for paying bird-dog bonuses for employee referrals should not just be to get great candidates, but to leverage your HR as PR, and to make everyone an ambassador for your organization. Get it?

As you go through each of the best practices, recommendations, and processes in the kit and on the CD, ask yourself what your intention or motivation is, and also what are the "other" benefits from or reasons for implementing that particular item. Discuss this with your leadership team; by doing this, you will start to become "big-picture" leaders *and* have greater motivation and commitment to see your initiatives through to success. Goals without action are just dreams!

As we have mentioned, the laws and regulations for human resources are constantly changing, so please be sure to check with us or with your own legal counsel when you are implementing a policy or process that may be subject to current or changing legal requirements. Healthcare and insurance reform legislation will create a lot of game-changers in the coming years, but the underlying principles and philosophies in this kit are evergreen and will be applicable in any environment.

Finally, you can actually speak with John or David, the authors of this kit, or one of their specialists, if you would like guidance or assistance in moving forward with any of these initiatives. In fact, you can even subscribe to their HRx Hotline for ongoing teleconsultation services as needed. This is a very cost-effective way to work through the process without the expense of a consultant traveling to you.

For more information, please feel free to call our toll-free HRx Hotline at 877-HRxHotline (479-4685) or e-mail John@FirStepInc.com, or 724-934-0272, e-mail djb@HCAdvisors.net.

Good luck!

Index

About the Authors

John Putzier, M.S., SPHR, is a best-selling author, and is the president of FirStep, Inc., a performance improvement consultancy founded in 1985. John is a noted expert on current and emerging workplace issues and trends, and a regular media source, appearing on CNN, NPR, and *ABC News*, and in the *Wall Street Journal*, *USA Today*, and many other publications.

John has served on the adjunct faculties of Carnegie Mellon University and Robert Morris University, where he taught human resource management and organizational behavior.

In 1994, John was awarded the highest lifetime certification, SPHR (Senior Professional in Human Resources), granted by the Society for Human Resource Management Certification Institute. He was the founder and past president of the SHRM High-Tech-Net and the National Speakers Association Pittsburgh. He has served on the board of directors of the Pittsburgh Human Resources Association, and as a judge for the People Do Matter Awards program.

As a professional speaker, consultant, trainer, and author, John is a sought-after presenter at conferences and associations across the country and around the world, and has even been invited to address the HR Summit in Singapore.

Through the study of demographics and psychographics, John always stays ahead of the curve on current and emerging workplace issues and trends. His presentation and facilitation style is direct, pragmatic, and sometimes even irreverent; however, his concepts and philosophies are rooted in sound organizational behavior and theory.

John can be reached by going to www.FirStepInc.com and clicking on "Contact Us" or by calling him toll-free at (877) HRx-Hotline (479-4685).

David J. Baker, M.A., SPHR, is a renowned expert in the field of human resources, and is managing director and CEO of HC Advisors, LLC (aka Human Capital Advisors), an HR consulting firm that specializes in implementing turnkey HR solutions. Dave developed his expertise by implementing HR operations in small to medium-sized companies, having served as the human capital partner for one of the largest venture capital firms in the country and creating the HR function in five national firms over the past 20 years.

Dave has been a guest speaker at numerous colleges and universities, including the University of Pittsburgh, Duquesne University, Saint Francis University, Clarion University, Carlow University, Chatham University, and Saint Vincent College, and has presented his "Hidden Secrets to Job Search Mastery" workshop to more than 3,000 people.

In 1993, Dave was awarded the highest lifetime certification, SPHR (Senior Professional in Human Resources), granted by the Society for Human Resource Management Certification Institute. He has served on the boards of the Pittsburgh Human Resources Association, McGuire Home, and the Pittsburgh Venture Capital Association.

As a consultant, professional speaker, career coach, and HR expert, David has presented his unique perspective on a variety of HR topics at numerous conferences and workshops. His HR "Concierge Service" brings together some of the most talented service providers in the country, from employment lawyers and headhunters to executive coaches, trainers, and insurance brokers—a network of world-class experts. There isn't anything that this team hasn't seen or solved.

He can be reached by going to www.HCAdvisors.net and clicking on "Contact Us" or by calling (724) 263-5773.